# It's Okay to Laugh

**Humorous Stories from the Disability Community**

**Presented by Oak Wealth Advisors**
**Foreword by Ryan Niemiller**

LITTLE CREEK PRESS
MINERAL POINT, WISCONSIN

Copyright © 2025 Oak Wealth Advisors

All rights reserved. No part of this publication may be reproduced, distributed, or transmitted in any form or by any means, including photocopying, recording, digital scanning, or other electronic or mechanical methods, without the prior written permission of the publisher, except in the case of brief quotations embodied in critical reviews and certain other noncommercial uses permitted by copyright law. For permission requests or other information, please send correspondence to the following address:

Little Creek Press
5341 Sunny Ridge Road
Mineral Point, WI 53565

ORDERING INFORMATION
Quantity sales. Special discounts are available on quantity purchases by corporations, associations, and others. For details, contact info@littlecreekpress.com

Orders by US trade bookstores and wholesalers.
Please contact Little Creek Press or Ingram for details.

Printed in the United States of America

Cataloging-in-Publication Data
Names: Mike Walther, Randi Gillespie, authors
Title: It's Okay to Laugh: Humorous Stories from the Disability Community
Description: Mineral Point, WI Little Creek Press, 2025
ISBN: 978-1-967311-68-2
Categories: BIOGRAPHY & AUTOBIOGRAPHY / People with Disabilities
FAMILY & RELATIONSHIPS / Children with Special Needs
HUMOR / Topic / Marriage & Family

Book design by Little Creek Press

We dedicate this book to families like our own,
who find humor in the journeys that they are on
with their loved ones with disabilities.

*The team at Oak Wealth Advisors*

# Table of Contents

Foreword by Ryan Niemiller . . . . . . . . . . . . . . . . . . . 1

Miracles and the Ministry of Laughter . . . . . . . . . . . . 5

Challenge Accepted . . . . . . . . . . . . . . . . . . . . . . . . 9

Oops! Did I Say That Out Loud? . . . . . . . . . . . . . . . . 12

Disability is Our Superpower . . . . . . . . . . . . . . . . . . 21

Disability: The Gift That Keeps on Giving . . . . . . . . . . . 33

Sibling Rivalry: The Disability Edition . . . . . . . . . . . . . 39

When Life Gives You a Disability, Become a Tech Wiz . . . . . 47

Just One More: Collecting Curiosities . . . . . . . . . . . . . 52

Mealtime Madness . . . . . . . . . . . . . . . . . . . . . . . . 58

Teaching with a Twist:
Supporting Students with Superpowers . . . . . . . . . . . 62

The Working Life: A Comedy of Errors . . . . . . . . . . . . 70

Hygiene Follies . . . . . . . . . . . . . . . . . . . . . . . . . . 74

Love, Sex, and Disability . . . . . . . . . . . . . . . . . . . . 78

Disability in the Community . . . . . . . . . . . . . . . . . . 81

The Hilarious Adventures of Traveling with a Disability . . . 89

Celebrations: When Disability and Chaos Collide . . . . . . . 96

Performances That Were Not Always Award Winning . . . . 100

# Foreword

By Ryan Niemiller

There is an old saying that goes: "Laughter is the best medicine." Though I would argue that penicillin or aspirin are far better treatments if you are ill, laughter is easily in the top three. Not to get too new-agey, but laughter is good for the soul. Finding something to smile at can be a lifesaver in a world where it is easy to be completely overwhelmed by negativity. I am living proof of this.

Society tries to teach us that certain realities of life are not funny. Certain realities of life that society tries to teach us are not funny. Disabilities, for instance, cannot be funny, right? I mean, just think of those poor, handicapped people. Their lives have to be so miserable. What joy could someone with a disability possibly have? Well, a whole bunch, it turns out. As a professional comedian for nearly twenty years and an amateur handicapped dude for forty-two, I can tell you for a fact that disabilities can be, and objectively are, funny. It's all about getting people to laugh with you, not at you.

I have a limb difference in my arms, a condition I have had since birth. People don't always understand that those with disabilities are more than their actual ailment. If you only paid attention to societal norms, you would assume individuals with disabilities across the board are inspirational. There is a thought that if you see someone with a disability out in the wild, their sole purpose is to make able-bodied people feel better about themselves. For me, if I inspire you, it is an accident. I didn't get into comedy to inspire the masses—I got into it because I'm an attention whore. We are not here exclusively for you but for ourselves. Sometimes that does mean inspiring. Other times it means breaking all of your preconceived notions of what people like us are. Trust me, when my wife tells me to take out the trash, but I can't be bothered because I am busy thinking of quippy responses to the ignorant things people say about my arms, she's definitely not inspired by me.

I have become comfortable with my disability, but that doesn't mean it isn't tough sometimes. I always explain it like this: I love video games, but if I were a video game create-a-character, I would not have chosen this template. To be honest, my disability can wear me down sometimes. But I try to live by the philosophy: "It's okay to be mad, but it's not okay to stay mad." I still have my rough days, even after turning my disability into a successful career. It still isn't fun to be stared at in public by children or have the server at a restaurant only speak to your wife because they assume she is taking out her brother with special needs. But it is really fun to then give her a long passionate kiss in front of the now disturbed waiter. It's about finding those little things that keep us going.

But having a disability is fun too. The potential for chaos and mischief is nearly endless. I have pretended my hand was being crushed during a handshake. I have gone into a nail salon and asked if I could get half price. When I see children staring at my arms, I sometimes pretend to be discovering them for the first time too. Is this mean? Maybe. Does this make people uncomfortable? You bet it does. But at the end of the day, it is funny, and there is joy in that. Life is hard—for everyone. But even when life is hard, we can get through it if we find something to smile about.

Humor is the great equalizer. We all would be a little better off if we learned to laugh at ourselves and the stuff that makes us unique. I am not sure what my fate would have been without a sense of humor. I grew up in a tiny town in Indiana, where I was the only person with anything like my physical differences. It was a recipe for disaster. I learned, however, that I was way better at making the jokes than anybody else. Everybody likes to laugh, and I was able to find a way to take something that could have been a hindrance and turn it into an advantage. I have since gone on to have a long career in comedy, placed third on *America's Got Talent* Season 14 in 2019, and, ironically, ended up inspiring millions of people anyway. Not too bad for joking about something I'm not supposed to joke about.

As you read this book, I want you to remember that these stories are not meant to garner pity. Enough people will try to do that in our everyday lives, and we don't want it. People often mistake us making jokes about our disabilities as making fun of ourselves. In my jokes about my arms, I am the hero of the story. We make the jokes as an act of empowerment, taking back control of a bad hand that has been dealt to us (pun intended). This book is meant to elicit joy and hope and give you a big old belly laugh. Those of us with disabilities are survivors. We are capable of so many great things. These stories will show you that we can love, we can inspire, we can frustrate, and hopefully, we can make you laugh. Once you've finished reading these stories, I hope you try to find the humor in life as much as you possibly can. The world is filled with turmoil and uncertainty, but there is a silver lining if you allow yourself to see it. You're going to have a blast reading it. And if you don't? Well, that's a hate crime.

# Miracles and the Ministry of Laughter

**Stuart is a seventeen-year-old nonambulatory with cerebral palsy, and Jake is his twin brother with autism.**

We are fortunate to have a church that is welcoming to our sons who both have disabilities. They are identical twins, and we have dressed them similarly for much of their lives. We often receive compliments about how nice they look.

One Sunday, both boys were with us at the service and were seated next to my wife, my daughter, and me. Stuart, who uses a wheelchair, was on the aisle and his brother Jake was having a hard time staying in place and wandered a bit during the service. Following the service, we decided to stay for snacks and fellowship with the other congregation members.

During fellowship, both boys were sitting next to my wife and me on a long couch. We left the boys on the couch to get some coffee and catch up with friends. While we were talking with our friends, we noticed Jake climbing into Stuart's wheelchair. He was having fun wheeling around the gathering space.

We were getting ready to leave when Jake suddenly jumped up from the wheelchair and started walking down the hallway.

Our friends and others in the congregation stared at him in disbelief. Then, someone shouted, "It's a miracle. He can walk!"

If only …

### Ryan is a seven-year-old with Down syndrome.

Ryan was seven years old when he went through First Communion. He completed the training and was very prepared. On the day of his First Communion, he dressed up in his suit. His grandfather was there. All the families were there, celebrating their children's First Communion. Each child went up with their family to take First Communion. When it was Ryan's turn, he didn't want to go, but we walked him all the way up to the priest at the altar. As the priest offered him the First Communion, Ryan said, "No, thank you. I'm full!"

### John is a sixteen-year-old with Down syndrome.

We were at church on Sunday morning, and toward the end of Mass, the priest said, "Peace be with you," to which we responded by shaking the hands of fellow parishioners or giving them a wave. However, John likes getting up close and personal with the other people, so he gave an older woman a huge bear hug and told her that she was a princess.

During the recessional, the priest was shaking the parishioners' hands. John shook his hand and said, "You're the man!"

The priest responded, "No, Jesus is the man!"

### Tessa is a sixteen-year-old with Down syndrome.

Tessa participated in a special religious development program called SPRED with her friends for many years. While there, she also enjoyed spending time with the church volunteers.

After completing the program, it was time for Tessa and her friends to be confirmed. The confirmation took place in the local church with the families of the individuals with special needs, the church volunteers, and those from the SPRED program.

When it was Tessa's turn to receive communion during the Mass, she walked up to the priest, looked back at her parents, and said, "I don't like to put that thing in my mouth."

Instead of putting the communion host in her mouth, she took it in her hand and proceeded to hand it to her mother when she returned to her seat and said, "This does not taste like a cookie."

When it was over, pictures were taken of everyone together, and Tessa started dancing and twerking on the pulpit, shouting, "I did it! I'm free!" I noticed the priest smiling and laughing. I'm still not sure if he was smiling and laughing WITH her or AT her!

**Liam is a twelve-year-old with Down syndrome.**

Liam was getting ready for First Communion, and we had weekly classes. Because of COVID-19, we stopped sending him. Then my father-in-law was ill, and we had to go to China, so Liam couldn't be part of the First Communion group. The priest wanted to meet Liam separately to ensure he was ready. The priest was telling him how special he was, and that Jesus loves him. Liam saw a statue of Jesus and walked over to it while the priest was telling him how loved he was and kissed and hugged the statue. He then began singing, "Amen, amen, amen ..."

We were also happy knowing Liam understood his role. You could see in Liam's face his adoration and how happy and loved he was. The priest also saw Liam's adoration and said he already had his own relationship with Jesus.

**Jake is a twenty-year-old with autism.**

Our son, Jake, stayed with his grandparents for the weekend. On Sunday morning he went missing. My parents, their neighbors, and the police searched for him for one hour until they discovered he had been sitting reverently in the chapel down the street enjoying the services. Thankfully, someone from the congregation called the police to see if there was a missing person and reported seeing him. As his dad, my first thought was, *I hope he is dressed and wearing clothes*—and he was! I'm pretty sure Jake was very happy with all of the hoopla AND the police presence while he was briefly "missing."

# Challenge Accepted

**Jason is a nonverbal twenty-three-year-old with autism. Even at an early age, he was able to find his voice.**

When Jason was little, I would sing "Twinkle Twinkle Little Star" to him before he fell asleep. He was involved in so many therapeutic sessions on a weekly basis, including speech, and nothing was really working. His language was not getting any stronger. I have a terrible voice, but I would sing to him. That night, I thought, *I am so tired from all these therapies*, and out of exhaustion, I just stopped singing the song. I could not believe it, but Jason finished the song! I started crying. He understood everything! I was so shocked and happy.

**Dave was a six-year-old with autism. We were told he would never walk or talk due to his challenges.**

My father longed to be a race car driver. Instead, he worked in a profession that allowed him to be home and support our family in a more stable fashion. That being said, he never missed an opportunity to drive like he was in a race. That included times when we were together in our large family sedan with front lap belts and no safety restraints in the rear seats. One afternoon in the 1970s, when our family of four was driving in our Oldsmobile

Ninety-Eight down the expressway, my father needed to take an off-ramp to connect to a different expressway. Our car was approaching the turn at or above the posted speed limit. As soon as my father entered the corner, all four tires began squealing as he worked the wheel to keep the car on the road. With no restraints, I slid toward my brother, and he slammed up against the door. For a split second, everyone was silent, holding their breath.

Then, out of nowhere, my brother yelled, "Jesus Christ!" The kid who was not expected to talk and had few words in his vocabulary, screamed a phrase he had heard before. His pronunciation, energy, and timing were all perfect.

I began to laugh. My father had a smile on his face, and my mother yelled back at him. "Dave, we don't talk like that!"

I interjected, "Yes, you do, and apparently, he knows more words than you thought he did."

## Brett is a three-year-old with cerebral palsy.

Our son, Brett, was diagnosed with cerebral palsy, right spastic hemiparesis, at sixteen months of age. He was immediately prescribed physical, occupational, and speech therapy and was fitted for an AFO and SMO (ankle foot brace).

While the physical therapy was to help improve his gait and balance and the occupational therapy to improve the strength and dexterity of his hand, the speech therapy was designed to hopefully improve his communication skills. The doctors told us due to the area of the brain damaged at birth, he might not be able to speak. The best thing for us to do would be for me, as his mom, to start taking sign language classes so I could then teach him and the rest of the family. Several months later, while still basically nonverbal, he had a huge breakthrough in one of his speech sessions. While his therapist was reading a picture book with him, he suddenly pointed to the picture of a little boy who had ripped his pants while jumping over a fence and loudly pronounced very clearly, "Grandma fix!" We were so thrilled he could talk and that he understood the communications around him. You see, his grandma, our family angel, spent a lot of time with us, and Brett had picked up on the fact that his mom could not sew, but his grandmother was our seamstress. Brett continued to improve with each session. My dear mom was always so pleased with his progress, especially because his first words were, "Grandma fix!"

# Oops! Did I Say That Out Loud?

**Tony is a fifteen-year-old with autism who likes to share his thoughts in a very open and honest way.**

No matter where you take Tony, he'll give you, the outing, or the experience, a score. For example, if you take him out to lunch, a movie, a park, or anywhere, you'll get a score. I should know not to ask at this point, but I do because I can't help myself! I'll ask Tony, "From a zero to ten, how was that?" and he will give me an honest answer.

"That was a four."

"A four? Why was it a four?" Tony would then tell me why he did not enjoy it, and he would be brutally honest and say that it was boring, it wasn't fun, it was too complicated, or it was too hot. He would spare you nothing. After a recent outing, I scored a seven and thought I had won the lottery. I was so excited about my high score! He is very funny, honest, and direct!

**Collin is an eight-year-old with epilepsy and a brain tumor.**

Our oldest son was diagnosed with uncontrollable epilepsy and a brain tumor. While in the hospital one weekend, the head coach of the Chicago Bears at the time, Coach Wannstedt and his assistants were visiting the kids the Saturday before their Sunday home game. When he came into Collin's room and introduced himself, our son turned to his dad and said, "Hey, Dad, didn't you tell me that the Bears stink?"

**Tessa is an eighteen-year-old with Down syndrome.**

I overheard Tessa on the phone with one of her teachers. When she was getting ready to hang up, she said, "Goodbye. I love you more than my mom."

**Ryan is a nine-year-old with Down syndrome.**

We were all hanging out in the living room while Ryan was playing one of his sports video games, and he missed a basketball shot. We were not paying all that much attention to his game until he missed the shot and screamed an expletive!

We looked at him and said, "Ryan, what did you say?"

And he said, "Shit, I missed the shot." His mother and I were quite proud of him because he used the expletive correctly.

**Jen is a twenty-two-year-old with Down syndrome.**

Jen's grandfather had a stroke due to his diabetes, and as a result, he would become sick and throw up while eating. He was always embarrassed by this, but we just dealt with it as a family. One night he was over for Sunday dinner, and everyone had left the table except for her grandfather, who was eating his dessert. Jen came over to the table with her bowl of ice cream and noticed that her grandfather was starting to throw up a bit. She looked straight at him and said, "You know, Grandpa, I am a little grossed out so I am going to take my ice cream and eat it in the kitchen."

She just got up and left the table. It was such a perfectly honest response!

### Tessa is a seventeen-year-old with Down syndrome.

I woke up on Mother's Day 2022 with my daughter, Tessa, patiently waiting and watching over me so she could give me a beautiful hand-decorated card she had made in school.

I thought to myself, *This is such a sweet gesture and probably the only one I will receive,* as I was certain my son probably forgot it was Mother's Day. I was going to do my best to make sure Tessa knew how special her card was to me.

Once I read the card, I looked at her, gave her a hug and a kiss, and thanked her. She turned to me and said, "Now leave me alone the rest of the day." She then walked out of the room laughing like she just told the funniest joke ever.

### Eric is a sixteen-year-old with Down syndrome.

Eric is very chatty and is not shy about starting a conversation with a complete stranger. One day we were at Walmart checking out, and he was talking to the customer behind us. I was not really paying attention because I was loading items onto the conveyor belt, and the lady behind us said, "Hi, what's your name?"

And Eric replied, "I'm Eric."

I turned around and said, "Hi, nice to see you," to the woman and continued to do what I was doing.

Eric continued talking to the woman and said, "I am SUPER excited."

The woman indulged him and said, "Really? What are you excited about?"

"My mom is going to have a baby!!"

That caught my attention! I whipped my head around and caught the expression of the woman who could clearly see that I was older than childbearing age.

But she excitedly said, "Congratulations!"

I very quickly shut it down and said, "No, no, no, no, no. I'm done having babies. Too old!" I then said, "Eric, you don't tell stories that are not true. Why did you say that?"

He then said, "I don't know, I want another brother!"

## Anna is a fifteen-year-old with Down syndrome.

Anna and I are always jamming out to music and singing in the car. We were in the car one day, and although my daughter loves to sing, she cannot sing well. She changes the words to the song, makes up her own lyrics, and cannot hold a tune. She is awful. While in the car, Anna had the nerve to say to me, "Can you please stop singing? You are not good!"

I smiled and thought, *If you only knew ...*

## Sophie is an eighteen-year-old with Down syndrome.

Sophie's friend had just received her driver's license and wanted to take Sophie out for ice cream after school. When her friend arrived at the house, Sophie congratulated her on getting her license and then said, "Take me to the bar. Screw the ice cream ... I want a drink!"

## Jenna is a nineteen-year-old with Down syndrome.

Jenna worked in a nursing home for many months as part of her transition program. So when Jenna's friends wanted to take her to a different nursing home to visit their grandmother one afternoon, we thought she would be comfortable and appropriate in that setting.

At the end of the visit, Jenna hugged the grandmother and said her goodbyes. As she was leaving the room, she turned around and said very loudly, "I hope you don't die!"

It looks as though Jenna may need some additional sensitivity training so that she can continue working at the nursing home! We want her to continue working at the nursing home!

**Sam is a sixteen-year-old with autism.**

One of Sam's favorite game shows is *The Price is Right*. At the beginning of the show, they call the contestants down from the audience with a specific phrase.

After my father passed away, we were at his funeral. It was before the service, and everybody gathered in the room awaiting the delivery of the casket. Sam decided to get up and go to the speaker's lectern in the front of the room and say, "Come on down!" Many people who knew Sam were laughing, but many others were very confused.

My mother, who was clearly grieving, thought it was the funniest thing and said, "Your grandfather would have loved that!"

**Peter is a five-year-old with autism and a brain disorder. His experience is proof that anything can happen in church!**

Peter is hyperlexic and a gestalt language learner. We received his diagnosis prenatally of complete agenesis of the corpus callosum, so he was in early intervention pretty much since he was born. That meant that at twelve months old, he had an evaluation that told us he had no pre-language sounds and was at extreme risk of being nonverbal. We started weekly speech and language therapy sessions with a therapist right away! He continued not speaking, until one day in church, in the middle of the sermon, he broke out with his first word—and first sentence: "I love my penis!" Luckily for us, the congregation was able to laugh with us and celebrate with us that Peter was speaking.

**Sam is a six-year-old with autism.**

When Sam was six, my husband, Dan, and I were shopping at Target. As we were putting our items on the belt to check out,

Sam took off walking toward the grocery section of the store. Dan trailed behind him to make sure he didn't get lost. Sam walked through the fresh food aisle toward the wall of frozen foods, where he saw a larger woman. She happened to be bent over. Sam decided to go right up to her and whacked her on the butt! My husband was furious and began profusely apologizing to the woman.

The woman rose slowly, looked at Dan, then down at Sam, and said, "Oh, honey, it's okay. It has been a while!"

## Dave is a seven-year-old with autism.

When Dave was younger, he had not yet been diagnosed with autism because that diagnosis was still twenty years away from being commonly acknowledged. In the absence of the diagnosis, we were learning that he was intelligent despite relatively significant delays in his language development. Although his language came slowly to him, his understanding of appropriate language took a bit longer.

On one occasion, while shopping for shoes, the heavyset salesman helping us was straining to reach down to tie my son's shoes. As soon as the salesman's head rose up to ask about how the shoes felt on his feet, my son said, "I think you are fat."

We bought those shoes without him trying on the other pairs that were brought out for consideration. That night, we spent some time discussing how saying something like that might hurt someone's feelings.

Maybe a month later, we were in a pharmacy together. While waiting in line to pay for our purchase, he noticed the woman in front of us was stooped forward and had white hair. His first words of engagement with her were, "I think you are old."

Once again, we spent another night discussing what is appropriate to say, or not to say, when talking to a stranger.

## Dave is a seven-year-old with autism.

When my son was in second grade, his school held a Christmas party for the children in the special education program that spanned kindergarten through sixth grade. Given how busy Santa Claus is in the weeks leading up to Christmas, one of the teachers had dressed up in full Santa garb. As soon as he walked into the room, my son walked up to him and exclaimed, "You are Mr. Edwards, not Santa!"

## Daniel is a twenty-three-year-old with autism.

As the receptionist for the past ten years at a special recreation association, I have fielded a lot of interesting calls from participants.

I have found that even if participants already know the answer to their questions, they often still call to inquire about the programs and events that are scheduled for the upcoming week.

In the past, I have accidentally shared incorrect information, and they have NO problem correcting me. They are not very kind about it. Many of our participants know every single detail about their program and even programs they are not signed up for because they study the program guide and know everything that is in it! They ask when and where the bus will be picking everyone up, and if I give a wrong time, they correct me over the phone. They want details on transportation, who the program leader will be for the class, and what type of snacks will be provided.

Daniel calls every Monday to confirm the program dates and times he signed up for that week. One Monday, I gave incorrect information to Daniel, and he replied very loudly over the phone, "You are wrong!" And then, without any hesitation, he proceeded to share every detail of the event he was asking about to prove that he knew more than me. I have come to the realization that the majority of the individuals, including Daniel, are simply testing me, which is humorous and also causes me some anxiety!

## Cathy is a twenty-two-year-old with Down syndrome.

We had updated the family in a family text that the Queen of England had recently died. Cathy, who was a fan of the band Queen and knew Freddie Mercury had died, asked, "What other band member in Queen died?" Queen was her favorite band, and she was perplexed when she heard the queen recently died!

## Sophie is a seventeen-year-old with Down syndrome.

I missed a call from Sophie and realized she left me a voicemail. Her message started by saying, "Mom, where are you? Pick up the goddamn phone now, and hurry up!"

## Emma is a fifteen-year-old with Down syndrome.

It was Down Syndrome Awareness Month, and we typically "celebrate" by putting up Down syndrome awareness signs in our yard. This year, I planned on recording Emma saying something positive about the month and what it means to her. I started recording and said, "Go ahead."

She said. "It is Down Syndrome Awareness Month. Don't be an asshole!"

## Jenna is an eighteen-year-old with Down syndrome.

Since turning eighteen, Jenna has not been shy about speaking her mind. She had a doctor's appointment the other day, and the doctor was running very late. Jenna was very annoyed. When the doctor finally entered the room, she said, "Nice of you to show up."

## IT'S OKAY TO LAUGH

**Tessa is a sixteen-year-old with Down syndrome.**

Below are Tessa's hilarious responses when asked three different questions.

I asked Tessa to bring her laundry basket downstairs to the laundry room. She said, "Seriously? You are unbelievable."

I asked Tessa to bring me a Diet Coke from the refrigerator, and she brought me a bottle of wine. She said, "You need this more."

I overheard Tessa's brother ask, "How old are Mom and Dad?"

Tessa replied, "Mom is 103, and Dad is 58." I grounded both children following that conversation!

# Disability is Our Superpower

**Tessa is a nineteen-year-old with Down syndrome.**

Tessa lacks a lot of confidence and gets very nervous ordering from strangers. As a result, she has difficulty maintaining eye contact at restaurants. Typically, I assist her with prompting, ordering/saying thank you, and will even resort to bribery to get her to assert her independence.

Starbucks recently opened in our neighborhood, and Tessa was very excited. She had already been in three times with her sister and needed some assistance with her communication each time. The fourth time she wanted to go, I told her to go in by herself and use her debit card. I would remain outside looking through the front window. I'm sure this looked odd to people who did not know what I was doing. I saw my daughter just standing there until she saw me wave at her. Then I left and waited in the car. Two minutes, four minutes, eight minutes later, and she had not yet exited with her drink.

I went back to the front window and noticed an employee talking to her. I went in and stood behind Tessa. I heard this amazing employee giving her steps on how to order a drink and encouraging her to do it by herself. The employee saw me, winked at me, and then brought her back to the counter, and she went behind it to take her order.

Tessa was wiping tears away from her face and whispering to herself, "Mom is going to kill me. I cannot do this." The employee asked her what she wanted, and very, very softly, my daughter ordered her overpriced frozen drink. She then turned to wait for her drink, saw me waiting, and said very proudly and loudly, "I ordered and did it all by myself!" The staff behind the counter started laughing and clapping!

**Aaron is a nine-year-old with autism and cerebral palsy. The thrill of his house escape was replaced by the realization that his adventure would have to wait.**

Aaron got out of the house, and we looked all over for him around the backyard and the house but didn't see him. I started running through the neighborhood, panicking and asking neighbors if they had seen him. My neighbor actually discovered him stuck on the fence. He was trying to climb over the fence on the side of the house where there were a lot of trees and bushes, so he was hidden from the front main street. I think his muscles were probably about ready to give out. He was hanging on for dear life, shaking and making noises! When the neighbor approached Aaron and asked how he was doing before assisting him, Aaron said, "I'm fine. Just hanging out!" Needless to say, he was fine but never attempted to climb the fence again.

**Gary is a seventeen-year-old with autism.**

Our Special Gifts Theatre classes continued to meet virtually during the pandemic. During one of these classes, Gary got up from his computer and did not return for a few minutes. We called his mother to tell her that her son left the class without telling anyone where he was going. While the mom searched for her son in the house, the teachers heard water turning on. Gary had left the class, turned on the shower, and began to take a shower—during class!

He returned to his class a few minutes later. He interrupted the class and said, "I'm back, and I smell really good now!"

## Taylor is a nonverbal fifteen-year-old with cerebral palsy and a history of seizures.

My son, Taylor, has cerebral palsy and seizures, is nonverbal, and has some other health issues. Taylor has always had a great love of water—being in the water, a pool, shower, in the rain. Anything. So his therapist talked to us about getting him a spa, which we did, and he absolutely loved it. You could hardly get him out on any given day. He would stay in it rain or shine, even in hot summers! He loved the sensation. He would spend two to three hours in that spa and got really comfortable in it.

For the first time, he went underwater. I thought he was having a seizure! I practically jumped in and pulled him out, and he was looking at me, really annoyed, like, "What's the problem?"

We had no idea that he could hold his breath and go underwater because he is so severely disabled. He was certainly able to share his feelings with us and how annoyed he was with us pulling him out of the water!

## Megan is an eighteen-year-old with Down syndrome who has a bright future as a bartender!

I created this monster! Megan wants to be a bartender, and she created an entire PowerPoint presentation that was part of her IEP meeting last year. With assistance, she added pictures of cocktails and beer for the presentation. During the IEP meeting, she told everyone she wanted to be a bartender so "I can make my mom drinks."

The teachers were all looking at me, and I said, "Let me explain!" I have a large group of friends from high school, and we went on our annual snowmobile trip. We rented a large house for our kids and us, and it had a big bar. After being outside all day we were having cocktails. Megan asked everyone if they needed more drinks, and everyone said yes. So Megan would get the drinks, crack open the beers, or pour some Vodka for everyone. Then one of the friends put out a glass, and everyone started to leave Megan tips. Over the course of the weekend, she made about sixty dollars!

Megan has no concept of money; whether you gave her a dollar or a one-hundred-dollar bill, she would say, "Best day ever!"

During the pandemic, I was working from home and on a Zoom call with some of my staff around one thirty in the afternoon. We were having an intense discussion. Megan walked into the kitchen and saw and heard our discussion. She proceeded to mix a drink and brought it over to me while I was on my Zoom call. I thought, *Please, for the love of God, do not come onto the screen and say, 'Hey, Mom. I made you a drink!'* I drank it because I obviously did not want it to go to waste. So, now, whenever she asks me if I am stressed, she's ready to make me a cocktail.

**Demetri is an eleven-year-old with Down syndrome who knows what he wants and how to get it.**

Demetri was sitting in the back seat of the car watching a movie with his headphones on when his dad stopped at the gas station. After his dad got gas, he got back in the car and proceeded to drive away. He noticed Demetri was not in the back seat and realized he had gotten out of the car. Demetri had hopped out of the car, went inside the gas station food mart by himself, and grabbed a blue Gatorade and a bag of chips without paying. He then proceeded to walk home by himself.

We had no idea he even knew how to get home on his own! Although his dad circled back to the store, he could not find him. Ironically, Demetri's older brother was driving by the gas station when he saw him walking alone. He picked Demetri up and went back to the food mart to pay for the Gatorade and bag of chips!

When Demetri was asked why he got out of the car and left, he replied, "I needed some alone time."

**Dana is an eleven-year-old with Down syndrome.**

Sometimes it is difficult to know when our daughter, Dana, who has Down syndrome, is playing us when she insists she can't do something that we know she can. Sometimes the trick to figuring this out is finding a powerful motivator. This motivator was food.

One night, I left homemade waffles in the refrigerator and told Dana they were there. Dana got up the next morning and made her breakfast using three skills she insisted she didn't have. First, she got a waffle out of the Ziploc bag. Second, she heated it in the microwave, and third, she cut it up with a butter knife.

Dana had insisted that she could not make her own breakfast and that she "needed" her mom's help all the time. The waffles seemed to have made divulging her secrets worthwhile, giving her more confidence and independence. With her new skills, maybe she can help make our breakfasts once in a while!

**Emma is a fifteen-year-old with Down syndrome.**

Emma had been in her room for some time when I knocked on her door to check in on her. I walked in, and she was on the floor putting items in her suitcase. Giggling to myself, I asked her where she was going.

She said, "The Wisconsin Dells."

Smiling, I asked her who she was going with, and she replied, "Myself. I am taking myself." I noticed she had packed her Curious George stuffed monkey, a swimsuit, socks, and pajamas. After a brief discussion on how she was planning on getting to the Wisconsin Dells by herself, she informed me she was going to "walk" to her destination.

For those who don't know, the distance between Chicago and the Wisconsin Dells is about two hundred miles. I asked her how she was going to pay for her hotel and food, and she said, "Mom can pay." When I told her I was not going to pay for her solo trip, and that walking was not an option to the Wisconsin Dells, she asked me if she could go to Mexico instead!

I told her we could consider it if I get to go too!!

## Hannah is a seventeen-year-old with Down syndrome.

There are mornings when my alarm does not go off, and getting the kids out of their beds on a school day is a struggle. As a result, there are days when they do not have time to eat breakfast or brush their teeth. "Shove a Pop-Tart in your mouth followed by a few mints" are the words that *may* come out of my mouth on a weekly basis.

On one such challenging morning, I found myself raising my voice like a drill sergeant. "Get your computers off the charging stations, get your shoes on, grab your lunch bags, and—"

Before I was able to complete my list, my daughter, Hannah, hollered back, "I am independent, I have Down syndrome, and I can do whatever I want!"

We had been talking to her about asserting her independence, so it was fantastic to hear her reaction!

## Tessa is a sixteen-year-old with Down syndrome.

Tessa loves to travel and stay at hotels. She believes anytime we stay at a hotel, it is one big party. Over Christmas, we were not planning on traveling anywhere and chose to stay home for the holidays. One cold December morning, I heard Tessa carrying something heavy down from her room. It was her suitcase. She was at the front door with her boots on, a winter jacket, scarf, gloves, and a hat. When I asked her where she was going, she replied, "Mexico."

I asked her why she wanted to go to Mexico this morning, and she said, "Because my home sucks. This place sucks!"

I then asked her how she was planning on getting to Mexico, and she replied, "I am going to walk."

I asked her what she packed in her suitcase, and she said, "None of your business."

I asked her when she was leaving and if she was going with anyone. She replied, "I am leaving now and going by myself."

I told her to have a great time, walk safely, and look both ways before she crosses any streets. I then opened the door for her, and she walked out. By the time I got from the front door to my back door, I saw her in the backyard, without her suitcase, swinging on the swing set. I guess Mexico will just have to wait!

## Olivia is a nonverbal nineteen-year-old quadriplegic with autism.

My family was at the outdoor shopping center, and I was pushing my sister Olivia in her wheelchair. We noticed a mother and her young son staring at my sister as we headed their way. The boy would not stop looking at Olivia, and he whispered to his dad and then continued to stare at her. My mom saw this and said to my sister, "Don't worry about it. Just ignore him." As the boy walked by us, Olivia put her arm straight out and hit him right in the head. He fell on the floor and started crying, but my sister laughed hysterically at what she did! We couldn't believe she did that.

My mom whispered to all of us, "No one messes with Olivia," we continued on with our shopping!

## Ben is an eleven-year-old with cerebral palsy and hypomyelination.

Ben's biggest fan is Ben. He loves himself and gets annoyed when people around town do not know him. He thinks everyone around him loves him. When he leaves one part of Georgia to go to another part of the state to visit family or attend a medical appointment, he does not understand why he does not get a warm reception from other people. He and his dad went to a doctor's appointment where he had been seeing the same doctor for years. New staff checked him into the appointment, and they did not know him. Ben was disappointed that the new staff did not give him a bigger hello or seem happy to see him, so without skipping a beat, while he was in his wheelchair, he said, "Hey, I'm Ben, and I'm awesome. You new people need to remember that!" They all started laughing hysterically! No filter and a great sense of self!

## Tessa is a sixteen-year-old with Down syndrome. Her mother may need to sleep with one eye open after she overhears Tessa's request.

Tessa went to bed angry with me. As she closed her bedroom door, I overheard her talking to herself: "Dear, God. Mom is not being nice to me. She took away my phone. Dear God. Please help me take Mom down."

I definitely slept with one eye open that night!

## Megan is an eighteen-year-old with Down syndrome.

When my neighbor Laura, a teacher, comes home in the afternoon around the same time Megan comes home from school, she'll see Megan letting her dog, Hunter, out in the backyard. The dog will want to hang out and play. Well, Megan is always yelling at the dog, and Laura is always cracking up because she hears Megan yelling and saying, "Hunter, get inside. I need to get into my pajamas and ree-ax." She is trying to say "relax," but she just can't pronounce it. I know I should correct her, but it makes me laugh.

That is her big thing after school: she needs to get into her pajamas right away and relax. And no one is allowed to bother her while she is watching her YouTube videos, especially those of Justin Bieber or Shawn Mendes. She gets really angry and tells us to leave her alone!

## Ben is an eleven-year-old with cerebral palsy and hypomyelination.

We traveled to Philadelphia for Ben's medical appointment. In bigger cities, you can order a van with a lift for a wheelchair, but for some reason, we always got stuck riding in disgusting vans with makeshift lifts from the 1970s that rarely worked. That was bad enough. Then, our Uber driver got lost leaving the airport! We realized this when he circled the airport for the third time. My wife was losing it in the back seat of the van and was super annoyed after the long travel day when my son very loudly said, "Why are we still at the f****** airport?" At that point, I gave the driver my phone with the accurate navigation to use to get us out of the airport and toward our hotel. Disability or not, my son's verbal skills are spot on—this is what advocacy looks like!

### Hannah is an eighteen-year-old with Down syndrome.

Hannah and I were at her doctor's appointment, and the doctor was running very late. Hannah was annoyed but occupied since she was playing on her phone. Then her phone died, and she became angry. After a forty-minute delay, the doctor came into the exam room with a huge smile and said, "Hi, Hannah."

Hannah replied, "Look who decided to show up!" I began laughing, but the doctor did not hear her, so I repeated what Hannah said.

I then followed up with, "She is eighteen now and has a voice. I would not keep her waiting next time!"

The doctor apologized and laughed.

### Liam is a ten-year-old with Down syndrome.

Liam is very clear about his therapy days when he works and his off days when he does not have anything scheduled. It took him a while to understand off days. Liam is constantly talking about how many days a week he needs to work to get his weekends free. His tenth birthday was coming up, and for Liam to be able to say, "It's my birthday. Call therapy—cancel. It is an off day!" was a huge milestone for us. The way he said it with his limited language was impressive.

### Tessa is a seventeen-year-old with Down syndrome.

During Down Syndrome Awareness Month, Tessa was asked to recite the Pledge of Allegiance at our village board meeting. She was super excited, and family and friends were in attendance to support her. When the village president called her up, Tessa said to everyone, "I am happy, and I can do this. I deserve a round of applause." So even before she did anything, she had the village board and attendees clapping for her. She then took her first bow of the night, followed by more cheers and applause from everyone in the room—again before she began to recite the Pledge. It was amazing to hear her advocate for herself and that people did what she asked them to do.

When they began reciting the Pledge, everyone expected Tessa to chime in and say it with them. What no one knew was that Tessa wanted to do everything without assistance. She thought she would be reciting the Pledge all by herself. I could tell immediately, as did everyone else, that she was super annoyed. During the Pledge, she said, "Guys, stop. What are you doing?" but no one stopped, and they finished the Pledge. She looked down and stomped her foot with her fists clenched like she was going into a fistfight with an opponent. Once done, there was silence, and everyone could tell she was irritated.

She then said, "It's my turn. I want to do it by myself and no one else. Okay, guys?" The village board and those in attendance agreed in unison, and Tessa began to recite the Pledge by herself. As she recited the words, she became much more confident and raised her voice.

At the end, everyone clapped, and Tessa took a well-deserved bow. As she began to walk away, she stopped and twerked. Yes, she twerked with a huge smiling face at the village board meeting. Everyone cheered and clapped one more time.

That's my girl!

### Craig is a ten-year-old with Down syndrome.

This is the value of my job, and this is why it's so great. I've been a recreation specialist for thirty years. At my first job there was a participant named Craig who had Down syndrome. He was on my golf team and in every program, but we connected through our love of golf. He and his parents asked me if I could help him learn how to rollerblade. I was twenty-four years old and was excited to help out. So, I arranged it with the family and the special recreation center. A new building was built at the time, so the parking lot was perfect for skating. We arranged that every Tuesday and Thursday night for the summer, we would get together for an hour, and I would teach him how to rollerblade. He learned and became a good skater, which was super fun for me, and it was a great experience.

Twenty-three years later, I saw Craig and his dad at a Special Olympics unified golf tournament. They came up to me, and his dad said hello. I said hi to Craig.

The first thing out of his mouth was, "Hi! I am still a great skater." Craig's dad said that he has continued to rollerblade every summer for the last twenty-five years.

# Disability: The Gift That Keeps On Giving!

**Ben is eleven years old and has cerebral palsy and hypomyelination.**

There's nothing more that Ben wants than to have a girlfriend. The problem is he's eleven years old and Alice, the girl he liked, was only nine. Alice was nonverbal and in a wheelchair. They went to day camp together. One day he came home from camp and said, "I want to write a love letter to Alice."

As his dad, I was super excited that he was being proactive and had these feelings because this is something that I didn't think would be possible when he was younger. His mom and I were not sure. So I wrote an age-appropriate letter to Alice on his behalf, and the next day at camp, he gave it to Alice's mom.

Alice's mom called me that night and was crying because it was such a lovely, beautifully written letter. She, like me early on, never thought that any boy would be reaching out and telling her daughter that they liked her. The next day at camp, Alice gave my son a best friend bracelet.

### John is a sixteen-year-old with Down syndrome.

John has a girlfriend who he says he loves, plans to marry one day, and will live together in his parents' basement. One day, his girlfriend stopped by the house to say hello, and John hid under a blanket the entire time because he was so shy and embarrassed.

Just as she was leaving, he ran after her, screaming, "I love you! Bye!" Their relationship may not work out if John continues to hide from his future wife!

### Megan is an eighteen-year-old with Down syndrome.

Megan has always been a creature of habit, sticking with a constant routine. Every night she had to have M&M's. We kept the candy in a container with a Cubs logo on it. She also had a specific bowl that only she could use. It was the tiniest little bowl because I only gave her seven or eight M&M's at a time. I liked to put some M&M's out for guests, so when people came over, Megan would always ask if they could put the M&M's in her bowl.

I was dating this guy for over ten years, and the only thing she missed about this gentleman was that he gave her a lot more M&M's than I ever did. Nothing else from those ten years resonated except that he gave her extra candy!

### Meghan is a seventeen-year-old with Down syndrome.

Meghan thinks whenever someone is nice to her it will become a relationship. Meghan was friendly with Jeremy, the captain of the football team. He was a cool dude and was very nice to her. He would always say hello to Meghan and make sure that she was okay. Of course, she started having a crush on him.

Soon it was homecoming, and they were all at the dance. Jeremy was dancing with his girlfriend, and Meghan went up to this girl and said, "You get away from him. That's my boyfriend!" It became well known that Meghan had a huge crush on Jeremy. He laughed it off and was very sweet and said he would finish his dance with his girlfriend and then dance with her. At that point, Meghan's paraprofessional interjected and made sure it was all okay. Jeremy handled it very nicely, but every time Meghan saw Jeremy, she'd make it known, "There's my boyfriend! There's my boyfriend!" because she was treated so well.

## Autumn is a seventeen-year-old with Down syndrome.

Autumn is a creature of habit and does not like to change her routine. When Autumn visits her friend Lilly's house, instead of simply knocking on the door or ringing the doorbell, she rings the doorbell about ten times and then runs off the porch to hide behind the big oak tree. Autumn calls this game "ding, dong, ditch, and hide-and-seek."

The funny thing is that Autumn has been doing this for the past three years. Lilly's family knows when they hear the repeated doorbell ring that it is Autumn. They pretend not to know who it is when they answer the door and always walk outside yelling, "Hello, anyone there?" while walking toward the big oak tree.

Lilly went to college out of state recently. Autumn still wanted to go to her house and play ding, dong, ditch, and hide-and-seek with her parents. So she did, and they answered the door and, as in past years, pretended not to know who was ringing their bell! The game continues!

## Liam is an eight-year-old with Down syndrome.

We went to the hospital for an appointment and noticed a guy had a gross-looking open wound on his leg. The girls were scared of the guy, but Liam went over and said, "Oh, you okay?

Okay?" He just wanted to comfort the guy.

In those instances when I'm only focusing on my child, it's interesting that Liam can look at other things around him, make observations, and notice that someone is not physically doing well and wants to provide comfort.

## Julie is a vivacious sixteen-year-old with Down syndrome who is definitely not shy.

Julie loves to ride her bike around town. She rides around the park and her neighborhood every day waving at people. Occasionally a train is backed up on the east side of the street. Much of the excess train traffic comes back on our street, in front of our home. Anytime she sees an abundance of cars in front of the house, Julie thinks that the cars are part of a parade ... for her. So when the train creates additional traffic on our street, Julie rides her bike up and down the street waving at everyone and saying, "Thanks for coming to my parade!"

Though she enjoys waving to anyone she sees on the street, she only talks to a certain group of people when she is riding. Whenever she sees teenage boys driving by or riding a bike, she will use her hand as a phone prop and scream, "Call me!" to the boys. Then she will giggle and laugh hysterically.

## Tessa is an eighteen-year-old with Down syndrome.

My daughter was unable to find me. I was at work and ran several errands without realizing my phone was turned off. When she could not reach me, she called her dad, who said, "Mom is at work."

My daughter called him a "liar" and then hung up the phone on him. She proceeded to get on her bike and look for me around town. She went to the three places she thought I would be: Walgreens, our local gym, and the grocery store.

One of my friends heard her at the grocery store, walking up and down the aisles, saying in a not-so-subtle voice, "Mom, where are you?" My friend Facetimed me with my daughter, and she said, "Mom, I found you. I am so glad you are alive!"

## Emma is a fifteen-year-old with Down syndrome.

Emma had her friend, who also has Down syndrome, over for a hang-out this past weekend. They played outside in the snow, had a snowball fight, and took a walk outside that lasted for twelve seconds! They were a bit bored when they came back in, so they played air hockey and attempted to steal candy from the candy jar without me noticing. I noticed the entire time because they were loud, giggling, and saying to each other in raised voices, "Be quiet. Don't tell Mom."

They ended up playing hide-and-seek in the house. Her friend was unable to find Emma after a few minutes of going up and down the stairs and checking the closets. I began searching for Emma along with her sister. Finally, I heard some giggling coming from the laundry room. I told her friend to open the door and look inside. When he did, he did not see her. We continued to hear laughter coming from inside the washing machine!! We all walked up to the machine and looked in, and there she was— inside the washing machine. She popped her head out and said, "Surprise!"

It's a good thing no one needed to start a load of laundry while she was hiding!

## Craig is a nineteen-year-old with Down syndrome.

I supervised our Special Olympics sports team, and every season we have a participant versus staff softball game. I was on third base, and one of the athletes came flying around the bases. I got down in my crouch position. The ball was coming, and I was ready to tag Craig. Instead, he slid, took me out, my feet went up and overhead, flying in the air, and we ended up on the ground together! I was so nervous that Craig got hurt, but as soon as we got ourselves together, he was able to stand and was laughing very hard. Craig said, "This is my favorite fun day!"

So many people think that individuals with challenges are so sensitive and can't get hurt or be put in uncomfortable situations. This proves the exact opposite!

# Sibling Rivalry: The Disability Edition

**Aaron is a nine-year-old with autism.**

Aaron and his older sister were at the kitchen table eating lunch. Aaron, who has limited verbal skills, was in a whiny mood. As he was carrying on, he kept repeating various things like, "Boo boo hurt" and "Check-up," which he had picked up from his *Sesame Street* "Elmo Visits the Doctor" video.

After listening to this for a while, his sister grew tired of his complaining, and she finally responded with, "Aaron, you do need a check-up—a check-up from the neck up!"

**Heather is an eight-year-old with autism who, like most siblings, becomes annoyed with her little brother.**

My daughter has autism and has spent two years working with a developmental psychologist to improve her social skills. Playdates now go well, and she has a group of friends that truly love each other. They're all equally quirky and wonderful and work through some of the bumps that come with not being able to read social cues effectively.

My son, who is a few years younger, also with autism, hasn't had the same experience yet and still struggles with controlling play and interacting with others. But he's also four and desperately wants to play with his older sister and her friends— just like every other four-year-old with an older sister! As he was stealing toys from his sister and their friends and running away screaming, my daughter looked dismissively at him and said to her friend, "Oh, don't worry about him. He has autism." It was one of those dismissive sibling moments where she wasn't thinking about a stigma related to autism or anything related, just telling her friend to ignore her annoying little brother and his "extra" behavior.

## Liz is a nonverbal ten-year-old with autism. The rougher the siblings play with her, the more she seems to enjoy it!

Liz has autism and is nonverbal. Our home has a large winding staircase that goes from the first to the second floor. When our parents were not home, all three of us siblings would have our own fun in the house. We put large couch cushions up and down the steps from the top to the bottom as padding. We all would wrap ourselves up, sit on a sledding saucer, and slide down the steps. Liz loved it the most, and I would get to push her down the steps as she sat on the saucer. She would laugh and smile all the way down. The other siblings would be there at the bottom to catch her, but we knew how much she enjoyed it because of her endless smiles and clapping and hugs that she gave us after each slide. When my parents came home, they knew something mischievous had been going on, but as long as Liz was not hurt, they did not mind the roughhousing with her!

## Dave is an eleven-year-old with autism.

Growing up in Missouri as an avid baseball fan, I rooted for both the St. Louis Cardinals in the National League and the

Kansas City Royals in the American League. My brother, Dave, who had multiple developmental delays and was later diagnosed with autism, has an amazing memory but not much interest in baseball.

In 1980, I was a teenager and was thrilled by George Brett of the Kansas City Royals, who was on the front page of the sports page regularly as he pursued hitting .400 for the season. Hitting .400 had not been achieved since Ted Williams hit .406 in 1941. Brett fell just short of the mark, hitting .390 for the season. His great performance that year led to the Royals making the World Series where they ultimately lost to the Philadelphia Phillies. Sadly, Brett was sidelined during the World Series with a painful bout with hemorrhoids. I was disappointed by the outcome of the World Series and that Brett was not able to play much.

The following spring, my family headed to Florida for a spring break vacation. Our timing worked out, and we were able to attend a few spring training baseball games. The highlight of the schedule for me was seeing the Royals play. My parents agreed to take my brother and me to the ballpark in the morning in the hopes that I could get autographs from a number of the players as they arrived.

The morning got off to a great start, with at least a dozen players stopping to sign cards or pieces of paper for me. I was thrilled! Then George Brett exited his car and headed toward us on his way to the locker room. I had special cards selected for Brett in the hopes that we would be able to get his autograph. I gave one to Dave, and I held the other one. As Brett approached, I asked if he would sign a card for both of us. He stopped and nodded that he would. My brother was silent. I handed the two cards to Brett. As he signed the first one for me, I was awestruck, and my heart was racing. He was handing the first card back to me when my brother, who had said very little all morning, exclaimed, "I think you had hemorrhoids!" I was terrified. He just insulted my hero at the very moment I was trying to get his autograph.

Brett was shocked, too. He asked, "What is his issue?"

I mumbled something about him having some disabilities, and Brett obliged with a second autographed card.

After waiting with the highest expectations for many months for the exact opportunity in Florida, my brother almost blew it for us. Over forty years later, those signed cards are among my favorites.

### Anna is a fifteen-year-old with Down syndrome.

Anna loves the TV show *Full House* and is infatuated with the character who plays Steve, the boyfriend. There is an episode where DJ tells her dad that she is going to marry Steve, saying, "I'm going to marry him; I love him, and there is nothing you can do about it!"

DJ proceeds to slam her bedroom door.

When Anna watches the show, she replicates the episode by yelling, "I am going to marry Steve, and I love him, and there is nothing you can do about it!" Anna then proceeds to slam her bedroom door. It is a shock to Anna when her siblings remind her that it is only a TV show, and it is not real. They also taunt her by showing her a current picture of Steve from the internet and that he is now a forty-six-year-old man and not the fifteen-year-old boyfriend in a TV series from many years ago!

### Megan is a nineteen-year-old with Down syndrome.

We had to put our dog, Hunter, down this past Friday, and it was absolutely horrible and so sad. We had someone come to give him the final shot to put him down. Megan was saying her final goodbyes following the final shot, and while crying,

I busted out laughing. Megan leaned over the dog, kissed him goodbye, and whispered to Hunter, "I know you are dead, but don't tell Jake that you are my favorite brother!" Jake is Megan's older brother!

## Demetri is a twenty-one-year-old with Down syndrome.

Demetri's older brother was recently diagnosed with non-Hodgkin's lymphoma. He has been getting excellent care and has begun his radiation treatment. A home health nurse stopped by our house to check on him and see if he or our family had any questions. The family was speaking to the nurse when Demetri walked into the room. The nurse, who was masked, looked up at him and said, "I know you!" Demetri's mom started asking the nurse questions about how she may know Demetri.

During this time, Demetri's brother, who HAS cancer, was patiently waiting for the nurse and his mother to return the focus of the visit back to him! The nurse figured out she had seen a photo spread of Demetri in the local paper documenting their high school homecoming dance. They all started laughing, and his mom began talking to her about the details of the dance. Again, all while his older brother continued to wait for the focus to shift back to his medical issues!

The family found this funny because loved ones with special needs typically take the focus and attention away from their siblings. They found it funny that the attention was taken away from the brother during his own medical crisis!

## Steve is a ten-year-old with Down syndrome.

When the children were younger, we were active in a support group that included mostly families with children with Down syndrome. Around the same time, Steve's brother, Alex, began to put together that his brother wasn't the same as other kids.

But considering all the families shared the Down syndrome connection, Alex once asked if ALL families had children with Down syndrome.

**Liam is a six-week-old with Down syndrome.**

We always say we won the lottery when we brought Liam home from the hospital, so we always call him our "lucky star." Following a six-week hospital stay at birth, he was sent home with a feeding tube. We took him to our church on the first Sunday home, and everyone came to bless him. They were selling raffle tickets, and we bought some in Liam's name. He won us a four-night stay in Lake Geneva! That is another reason we call him our lucky star; that nickname stuck with our family. Whenever we are looking for a spot in a parking lot or garage, his siblings always want Liam with them because they find better parking spaces when their lucky star brother is with them!

**Dexter is a fifteen-year-old with Down syndrome.**

Dexter's best friend is a Kermit the Frog stuffed plush toy. He's had him since he was seven, and Kermit pretty much goes everywhere with him. We also believe Dexter thinks Kermit is real because he will try to feed him. Kermit sleeps in Dexter's room on a little American Girl doll bed every night. Dexter loves Kermit but also can be very rough with him. He has thrown him in trees and dropped him out of the window at a drive-through.

My daughter goes to Loyola University in Chicago, and last year she took Dexter downtown to see her dorm room and see a Loyola basketball game. They walked along the lakefront to get from her dorm to the arena, and although she was holding Kermit, Dexter was able to wrestle him out of her hand. He took Kermit and threw him into Lake Michigan.

His sister said, "You killed Kermit!" and Dexter started to

cry. She Facetimed her mom and told her what happened. Her mom reminded her that they have a "backup Kermit" they call Kermilita.

Mom told Dexter, "Since you threw Kermit in the lake, he is now home resting because he is not feeling well, and you will see him when you get home."

The funnier part happened the next day. I asked her to see if Kermit washed up on shore or somewhere near the campus. She was walking along the Loyola campus lakeshore and saw little green legs sticking out behind some rocks. She saw Kermit's little feet poking up from the rock! We were unable to retrieve Kermit, but I thought it was really funny that he was found with his legs sticking up!

Since all of Dexter's family and friends knew how much he loved Kermit, we sent a story message out notifying everyone that the body of Kermit the Frog had washed up on the lakeshore campus, and the number one suspect was Dexter! It was fun getting them involved.

## Caroline is an eighteen-year-old with Down syndrome.

We have a very funny family, and we laugh and make jokes about ourselves daily. Caroline's younger brother was attempting to have a conversation with her during dinner one night. He became very annoyed when she refused to look at him or even acknowledge that he was trying to talk to her. He looked at me and asked, "Did you ever have a drink of wine or beer when you were pregnant with me?"

I replied, "No."

Without skipping a beat, he said, "Based on the fact that Caroline has Down syndrome and is refusing to look at me or respond to me, I assume you drank yourself silly when you were pregnant with her!"

**Autumn is a thirteen-year-old with Down syndrome.**

We received our Comcast cable TV bill and were shocked to see it was $800. Upon reviewing the bill, we noticed that twenty movies had been purchased. Not rented—purchased! There were not twenty different movies but rather two movies purchased ten times each. We had not shared the Comcast PIN with Autumn, so we were surprised to see that the *Tom and Jerry* and *Frozen* movies had been purchased.

We later found out that Autumn's older sister gave her the Comcast PIN but said, "Don't tell Mom and Dad I gave it to you. It is our sissy secret!" Fortunately, we were able to get our bill reduced by playing the "special needs card."

# When Life Gives You a Disability, Become a Tech Wiz!

**Sam is a sixteen-year-old with autism.**

Sam, our sixteen-year-old son, is a practical joker. He can do many things on the computer and has done so since he was young. We learned not to leave our phones or computers unlocked in his presence.

One of my favorites is Sam likes to sign us up for anything using our name and address. He also has a sense of humor. He once signed me up for a weight loss program and a bikini wax. That was really bold! One day my husband answered the phone, and it was someone from a community college asking if he would like to improve his capabilities and earning potential. Dan said, "What are you talking about? I do not need a community college to talk to me about increasing my earnings. I am a doctor and have my doctoral degree, and I got pretty far in school, but thank you anyway!" This was our Sam!

**James is a fifteen-year-old with autism.**

My son, James, loves sitting and watching YouTube videos on

his iPad, but it was dead. So my husband, Tim, gave James his cell phone so he could watch YouTube videos. James was happily sitting on the couch watching his videos, and my husband went over to help him. He realized that James was in the Lyft app and had ordered a driver to pick him up at the house! James somehow figured out how to get out of YouTube and into the Lyft app! We then realized the car was outside the house, in our driveway, waiting for him. James not only ordered a Lyft, but it was a really expensive XL. We saw a sleek black Chevy with black tinted windows.

The driver said it was scheduled to take a passenger to Opryland Hotel in Nashville, about thirty minutes from the house. I explained to him, "You know, I'm so sorry. Our son has an intellectual disability."

The driver chuckled and understood. He said there have been more bizarre stories like this and has experienced some funny things as a Lyft driver. I paid him for his time. I went back inside, and Tim and I had a good laugh.

I thought, *This is like the modern-day version of running away from home. This is what kids are doing now: they're ordering a Lyft and going to the nicest hotel they can think of, and they're just going to get away from their parents for a while!*

### Sam is a seventeen-year-old with autism.

Sam was seventeen years old. Although he has a wonderful sense of humor, he has some difficulty with the concept of money and how much things cost.

When Sam was in junior high school, I walked into his room, and he was on his computer looking at different things on eBay. I didn't know what he was looking at, but he was getting ready to send a bid of $1,000,000! Fortunately, we were able to stop him. We knew he had difficulty understanding how much things cost. It made sense that Sam wanted to order it, but not for $1,000,000. What did Sam deem worthy of this ridiculously high bid? A Thomas the Train cup, a five-pound bag of Swedish Fish, and a World's Best Dad mug!

You never know when Sam's online orders will show up at our house. The items are usually really funny and in response to something we might have mentioned, or he overheard us talking about it. His intentions are always to be funny and kind.

## Jackson is a twenty-year-old with Down syndrome.

My brother, Jackson, has Down syndrome, and ever since he was little, he has liked beads, specifically necklace beads. He does not like to wear them; he likes to run them through his fingers as a sensory thing. It calms him down. Whenever I go somewhere and see beaded necklaces, I always bring him back some. Well, he also really loves being online, on email, and snooping in other people's email that they leave open. If my family leaves their email and Amazon accounts open, he will order things. For a period of time, he would focus on cheap items that you wouldn't typically order through Amazon. He has ordered a two-liter bottle of Diet Coke and a king-size Reese's Peanut Butter Cup.

One time a package came in the mail, and my mom had to sign for the package because it was expensive. She could not figure out why she would have to sign for it. She thought it was a beaded necklace, but it wasn't. My mom had to sign for it because it was an $8,000 pearl necklace! Mom was so upset and started yelling at my brother, "This is not okay. Now we have to insure it and send it back." Then my dad came home, and my mom told him about the $8,000 necklace and wanted my dad to yell at him also.

My dad told my brother, "You can't do things like this, and who exactly did you even order the necklace for?" thinking maybe he ordered it as a gift.

My brother said, without flinching, "I ordered it for myself!"

**Sam is a sixteen-year-old with autism.**

One day, I got a call from my assistant, who had a few questions about my calendar. She asked me to look at a specific date because she didn't understand the entry. Sam had put the season premiere of the TV show *Deal or No Deal* on my work calendar. I told her my son must have done that when I left my calendar unlocked! The assistant thought I was just a really big fan of game shows! To this day, we still have no idea how Sam accessed my work calendar.

**Dylan is a fifteen-year-old with a dual diagnosis of Down syndrome and autism.**

Dylan has a history with phones and doing naughty things with them. When my oldest daughter first got her phone, we were walking along the Fox River in St. Charles. Dylan took her phone out of her hand and threw it in the river! He often takes my phone and hides it in the freezer. We always need to be cognizant of where our phones are.

I was in the kitchen with him and must have left my phone on the island. Dylan was making his breakfast, so after the microwave beeped, I went in to help him remove his breakfast sausages. Lo and behold, right next to the sausages was my phone! Dylan put my iPhone into the microwave along with his breakfast sausage and nuked it for a minute and a half!

Although the phone did not blow up in the microwave, I had to borrow my daughter's phone and have mine replaced two months later!

**Sam is a sixteen-year-old with autism.**

I was talking to a friend of mine, and out of the blue, he asked, "By the way, I love your family's website." I told him that we didn't have a website.

He then said, "Oh yeah, you do."

I said, "I would know if we had a family website." I looked, and there it was: a website full of pictures of us, links to different websites like The Weather Channel and Sam's favorite game shows, along with the names of our pets and their birthdays. There was also a calendar with our birthdays and different events. It was a very elaborate website, and we didn't even know it existed. We asked Sam to please make it private because some of the pictures were not that flattering.

# Just One More: Collecting Curiosities

**Dan is a twelve-year-old with autism.**

Supper clubs are big in Wisconsin, and Dan was obsessed with their cloth napkins. He would collect the cloth napkins of every supper club he went to and Sharpie marker the date and the name of the supper club he got the napkin from. He would be so excited when he went to a club and saw the cloth napkins. I would usually talk to either the host or the server, explain the situation, and tell them that I would pay for the napkin and ask them to put it on my bill. All the places thought it was so cute and adorable and would always bring a clean cloth napkin and not have him take a dirty one home with him.

Dan also collects keycards from hotels! If anybody we knew went anywhere, they would make sure to bring back a key card for him.

One of his teachers brought him back a keycard from her trip to Paris, and he was so excited. He still has the keycard from her hotel. He keeps these tokens as part of his memories of his past and where he wants to go when he gets older. When I asked if I could travel with him when he gets older, he responded, "No, thank you!"

## Dave is a sixteen-year-old with autism and is a huge golf enthusiast.

In the early 1980s, Dave was a teenager. He had developed a love of golf courses. That love led to him collecting golf scorecards. As a family, when we would drive past a golf course, we would stop and get a scorecard for him. When our family traveled, we would ask for one of the scorecards if there was a resort golf course near where we were staying. The collection began to grow rapidly as family friends and business associates learned of his collection and began making contributions.

Dave also had subscriptions to several golf magazines. While he would occasionally read the articles, his enjoyment was primarily in looking at the pictures of the golf holes and learning about new courses that would be opening. By the mid-1980s, his collection of scorecards began to number in the hundreds. As his collection grew, he created a script for calling golf course pro shops and requesting that they mail him one of their scorecards. That script worked well and helped him build confidence in communicating with strangers. Of course, his passion for adding to his collection also helped a great deal in overcoming his challenges with communication.

After a while, my parents set a budget for making long-distance calls around the country and told him that he could only call five golf courses per month. At that time, long-distance calls were much more expensive than making local calls. Dave would create a list of the courses he most wanted to add to his collection, and then he would reach out to those courses in order. My parents never interfered with his list and let him decide which scorecards he wanted most.

By the decade's end, he had collected scorecards from all the courses that held the major tournaments on the PGA and LPGA tours. Dave's process of collecting remained the same. He would contact the courses he most wanted to add to his collection, and the long-distance bill would usually be under fifty dollars a month.

Having collected over a thousand scorecards by the end of the 1980s, Dave's appetite only grew. However, my parents had grown bored listening to him when he shared the details about the courses he wanted to contact in future months. In retrospect, that was a mistake.

In one month, he called five courses and had rather lengthy conversations with each one. As it turned out, the extra-long calls resulted from the person on the other end of the line needing to find someone who could speak English. Many of the courses he called required multiple attempts as he would have people hanging up on him, and in other cases, he had to wait on hold for a while. All five courses were in Japan!

The long-distance bill that month approached $500.

Dave now has over 17,000 scorecards, and his collection continues to grow. Fortunately, domestic calls no longer incur long-distance surcharges, and his international scorecard desires have been mostly satisfied.

## Dan is an eight-year-old with autism who shares his fascination with combination locks with his peers.

Dan had many obsessions throughout his childhood and sometimes still does. In third grade, he had an obsession with locks and combination locks in particular. When he would do well at school, instead of getting ice cream or anything like that, we would go to Target, and he would pick out a new combination lock. He would commit it to memory without ever writing down the combination numbers. He would remember the combinations for big locks, small locks, any type of locks. At one point, he had about fifty of them.

One day, the school notified us that they were having a show-and-tell day. His dad and I were thinking, *What is he going to bring to class?* I remember as a kid bringing in a stuffed animal or something like that to share with the class at that age. Dan told us that he wanted to bring his locks. There were so many locks that Dan had an old white tool bag he would use to carry all of them. It probably weighed about twenty pounds. His dad and I were a little nervous because we could not be at school with him.

So we sent him to school that day with his locks and had no idea how it would pan out and what that would look like for him. Following the class and show-and-tell, we received a note from this teacher that Dan's show-and-tell presentation was the best ever because he explained his locks and what this one does and what that one does. His presentation became almost like a magic show for the kids. They all went up to him and ended up challenging him as they randomly all picked a lock—can Dan open this one? Each kid reached into the bag and pulled out a lock, and Dan was able to open it. They were so fascinated that he could do that, and they were like, "No way!" They thought it was the coolest thing ever that he could open any lock they put in front of him. It was a great experience for him and his peers.

### Dave is a sixteen-year-old with autism.

For much of my brother's adult life, he has had an obsessive-compulsive desire to collect certain things of interest to him. His interests have been golf scorecards and photos of airport runways. While collecting golf scorecards is a relatively straightforward endeavor, aerial photos of airport runways are not nearly as accessible. This story about my brother's passion occurred in the late-1980s, before the advent of the internet.

Through some good fortune, my father's law practice included relationships with some commercial aviation pilots. Once they learned of my brother's interest in airports, they would send him paper flight manuals and airport directories. He was thrilled. The books often included small diagrams of the runway layouts. After some years of memorizing all the lengths of the runways, his interest expanded to wanting photos of the more interesting airport layouts.

While he accumulated photos and postcards from many of the largest airports in the world, his desire for new photos continued to grow.

One summer, he was doing some part-time administrative work at my father's law firm, which bore his name. My brother had been prohibited from calling airports to request photos of runways after several months when our long-distance bill reached triple digits due to his excessive calling. Being resourceful, he found the law firm's letterhead and knocked out a letter requesting photos from a special California airport for which he lacked any photos or schematics regarding the landing strip layouts.

About a week after he launched the letter, the law firm receptionist received a phone call from California demanding that the caller be able to speak with my brother—immediately. The receptionist was initially shaken by the abruptness of the demand. Recognizing that my brother was autistic and the person calling had an angry tone, she instead put the call through to my father.

My father answered, and the caller insisted on speaking with my brother. My father explained that he would take the call for my brother, and the caller said, "Okay, hold for the general." Before my father could inquire about the reason for the call, the U.S. Air Force general demanded to know why my brother, the attorney who authored the letter, wanted photos of their military base and his intentions. After catching his breath, my father explained that my brother has autism, is not an attorney, and has an extensive collection of airport photos. He apologized repeatedly and assured the general that he would speak to his son and that he was sorry for the confusion caused by the letter.

The general relaxed after recognizing the lack of threat and asked about my brother. After a few more minutes on the phone, my father had been offered a tour of the base the next time my family was in California.

A year or two later, my parents took my brother to California. They made a point of contacting the Air Force base to arrange a tour. To their surprise, the general accompanied them on part of their tour, including their time on the tarmac. Within a few minutes, the general sent an order into a walkie-talkie and told my family to look to the north. Their eyes widened as the B-2 stealth bomber made a low-altitude pass directly over the base. While they couldn't hear the aircraft pass overhead, it was a sight they will never forget.

My brother returned home with a number of Air Force mementos, some great memories, and a photo of the runways.

# Mealtime Madness

**Sam is a sixteen-year-old with autism.**

One day I was working from home, and it was around eleven thirty when there was a knock on the door. I opened it, and it was Domino's Pizza with ten molten lava cakes. I said, "Can I help you?"

The delivery man said, "I'm here to deliver your online order."

I said, "We did not order anything from Dominos, and I think I would know if I ordered lava cakes."

He said, "Okay," and turned around and left with the cakes.

As the man left, I thought, *Sam did this*! Sam came home from school and just started laughing, and laughing, and laughing! Sam's online ordering skills are very impressive!

**Veronica is an eighteen-year-old with Down syndrome.**

Veronica is a creature of habit. Friday nights are always pizza nights at our house, and for the longest time, Veronica only liked cheese pizza. Since her brother, Jake, liked sausage, we always got half cheese and half sausage. We always encouraged her to try the sausage and thought she would like it, but she always thought it was gross. One time she tried it, and I said, "How about we just order a sausage pizza?"

She said, "No, Mom. I don't like sausage pizza. I like cheese pizza with sausage on it."

"Okay, I'll order that!"

Now she just calls it sausage pizza. But for the longest time she insisted, "I only like cheese pizza with some sausage on it."

### Anna is a thirteen-year-old with Down syndrome.

Anna and her dad were at the Wendy's drive-through and brought some dinner home for the family. When Anna opened her bag, she became very upset and said, "Dad got me a salad. I don't like salads." Her dad made it very clear that it was not a salad but a hamburger with a piece of lettuce on top.

### Maria is a twenty-one-year-old with Hurler syndrome.

Maria ordered from DoorDash for the first time after moving away from home. A week or two later, I checked the checking account and noticed an outstanding charge of eighty or ninety dollars. I asked Maria about it, and she confirmed she ordered a kid's mac and cheese and a small pizza for her roommate. After confirming she didn't put in multiple orders, we noticed the restaurant was thirty-five miles away! They really got us with the outside zone delivery fee! Note to self and Maria ... put restrictions on deliveries!

### Caroline is a seventeen-year-old with Down syndrome.

Everyone who knows Caroline knows that she has a sweet tooth and is happiest when she is eating sweets and desserts. There are times when all she talks about is food and what she is planning on eating for every meal. There are days when she texts me at ten thirty in the morning from school to ask me what we will have for dinner, or she will ask if she can buy a "special treat" from the school vending machine. She often calls me from school to ask if she can bake brownies after school or if we can have a family meeting when everyone gets home. The family meeting always consists of Caroline gathering everyone together and asking what is for dinner. If she does not like the answer, she will attempt to manipulate other family members into eating exactly what SHE wants, usually from a few of her local fast food restaurants!

### Autumn is a seventeen-year-old with Down syndrome.

My entire family, including nieces, nephews, aunts, and uncles—over twenty-eight of us—went to dinner at a very nice restaurant in June to celebrate a family member's graduation. The waiter approached the table and asked each of us what we would like to order for dinner. The waiter approached Autumn last. We thought that ending with her giving her order would provide her with a teachable moment on how to be patient.

The waiter bent down next to her and asked, "What do you want for dinner?"

She replied, "You sure took your sweet time getting to me, didn't you?"

### Anna is a fourteen-year-old with Down syndrome.

Joe and Anna were on their way home from Walmart with loads of grocery bags. Joe had promised to stop and get Anna a milkshake on the way home. The temperature was approximately 102 degrees, and our car died.

A passing police car stopped, and the officer felt bad that it was such a hot day. She did not want our groceries to go bad or make us wait for a tow truck, so she put everything in her police car and drove us home. While in the police car, Anna's main concern was not about the groceries spoiling or the car no longer working but that she had not gotten her shake.

She repeatedly stated in the police car, "I want my shake. You promised a shake to me." The police officer was tired of listening to Anna complain, so she actually stopped and bought her the milkshake she was promised!

Apparently a police officer's job is to protect and serve ... and buy milkshakes!

## Maria is a twenty-one-year-old with Hurler syndrome.

We were at a restaurant on spring break, and Maria wanted a daiquiri but forgot her ID. The server informed her he would be unable to serve her.

So she said, "Fine. Forget it. I'll have chocolate milk." Maria can certainly transition quickly ... alcohol to chocolate milk!

# Teaching With a Twist: Supporting Students with Superpowers

**Lilly is a seven-year-old with autism.**

As a teacher, some of my students show up to school with specific items they are attached to and become obsessed with. One would think that a stuffed animal is something that a child would bring to school if they are going through something or feel that they require extra support throughout the day. One day, Lilly showed up at drop-off with a large watermelon. When the car door opened, the watermelon rolled out of the car, smashing onto the ground and cracking open. The mother insisted Lilly would be fine as long as she had the rest of the watermelon by her side throughout the day. We took the watermelon inside the school and immediately threw it in the garbage. We kept Lilly very busy, and she was just fine without having to walk around the hallways with a large watermelon by her side!

**Jane is an eight-year-old with autism.**

I teach elementary school children with disabilities. They keep me on my toes. One day, Jane, who has autism and some behavioral challenges, was having a rough day. She was not listening, and she was unable to sit still. After texting her mother, the mom suggested some quiet independent time with some toys or puzzles. She indicated Jane had not slept well the night before, so maybe she just was tired and acting out. I brought Jane to the quiet resource room and shared some smaller puzzles for her to have fun with, as well as a few other items. I left the room but returned after a few minutes and noticed that one of the pieces of the puppy puzzle she had been working on had a bite out of it. When I asked her where the puzzle piece went, she said, "In my belly. I hate puppies!"

## Sarah is an eighteen-year-old with autism who was really tired during class!

During one of our virtual Special Gifts Theatre classes, a funny incident took place. Sarah was engaged and communicative during the class. The teacher called on Sarah for a response and noticed that her head was on the table. The teacher repeatedly called her name but still got no response. Her teacher then heard Sarah snoring—she had fallen asleep during class! We contacted her mother to let her know that Sarah had fallen asleep during class, and she was able to wake her up! Sarah was fine and continued to participate in class.

## Maria is a twenty-one-year-old with Hurler syndrome.

Maria goes to school at a "dry" campus, meaning alcohol consumption is not allowed. A few nights before she was off to school for the semester we had some family and friends over for dinner. Later that evening, she seemed quite nervous. She proceeded to share that she ate some beer cheese dip and didn't want anyone to find out, assuming it would disqualify her from continuing her program.

## Ryan is an eighteen-year-old with Down syndrome.

Ryan was graduating high school and was attending his graduation ceremony. Ryan does not like it when his last name is not pronounced correctly, but he knew the person saying the graduates' names as they crossed the stage knew how to pronounce his name, so it was fine. Except, that person got COVID-19 and could not attend, so there was a replacement. Ryan was on stage, ready to hear his name. His last name was pronounced incorrectly, and we could tell he was super annoyed.

Immediately, he screamed, "My last name is not BEAR. It is BAAR!" Everyone in the auditorium started cheering and clapping, loving that Ryan corrected the guy. Ryan received his diploma and was on his way to the end of the stage to have his picture taken. Most people stand and simply smile. Not Ryan. He twirled in front of the photographer and flexed his arms while posing for his picture!

## John is a seventeen-year-old with Down syndrome.

John had an amazing Earth Science teacher in school. The class was application-based, and early one week they began dissecting a pig.

Later that week, John and his mother were having breakfast. This was also around the time John was learning about sex, birth control, etc. John asked what a diaphragm was. His mother proceeded slowly for the next five minutes until it became obvious John was getting quite confused. She suddenly put it together that he was asking about the pig's diaphragm he had been dissecting in class!

After my wife put him on the school bus, I received a call from her, crying with laughter about what had happened.

## Steve is a ten-year-old with Down syndrome.

When Steve was in fourth grade there was a lot of interaction with parents coming into the school. One day I went to have lunch with Steve, and his paraprofessional pulled me aside and said she felt really bad about what had been happening in the home but wanted to let me know that it's always a good idea to keep the team updated on changes at home. I was very confused and asked her what she was talking about.

She said Steve had been outside crying over the last few days about his dad, who was a long-haul trucker, and that he had been working really long hours away from home. I heard this from the teacher, and my mouth gaped open in shock. She said she was sorry to hear that we were getting a divorce. But we should have communicated with the team because significant changes like this make for a difficult transition and problematic behaviors. I started laughing and said, "Where does Steve come up with this stuff?"

I told the teacher that my husband works less than fifteen steps away from me upstairs in his home office, he is not a long-haul trucker, and as far as I knew, we were not getting a divorce. Later that night, when Steve and his sister, Catherine, were together, I mentioned it to Catherine, and she told me that the story Steve told his teachers was taken from Steve's favorite cartoon, *Arthur*. In the episode, there was a truck driver who worked a lot and wasn't home. The son was sad, and the dad and mom were getting a divorce.

Steve takes these stories from TV or a movie and pretends the story is his as he is looking for sympathy for people. We always have to keep a close eye on Steve because I never know what story he is going to tell somebody!

## Jenna is a seventeen-year-old with Down syndrome.

While Jenna was in school, I received a text from one of her friends with an attached video. The text read: "I was in the lobby area and looked outside in the courtyard and saw Jenna sleeping on the bench." I looked at the clock and wondered why she would be outside, lying on a bench, by herself.

I immediately emailed her teacher, asking, "Why is my daughter sleeping on a bench in the courtyard during school hours?"

Although he did not get back to me right away, the friend who sent me the video approached Jenna at the bench and said, "Hey, Jenna. What's up? Are you sleeping?"

She looked up at her friend and said, "Oh, hey. I was tired after lunch and wanted to take a nap."

## Tessa is a seventeen-year-old with Down syndrome.

Tessa was in the first few days of her senior year of high school. She was excited to take her senior foods cooking class. Tessa loves to be in the kitchen baking, cooking, and eating! However, there are times when her behaviors impede her ability to be successful, and this is one of those stories.

She was in her first senior foods class of the year. The teacher had previously taught Tessa in two other cooking classes. Tessa sat down next to some of her friends, and when the teacher asked everyone to move to their assigned seats, Tessa did not move. Instead, she folded her arms and simply stared at the floor, uninterested in moving. Her teacher's aide attempted to be of some assistance but failed. The teacher reminded her a few times to follow the rules and get up. She did not. The other students had all moved to their assigned seats and were all encouraging Tessa to move. She did not.

On the first day of senior foods, she got kicked out of the

classroom for not listening and following directions. The teacher called me to let me know what had happened in class and why my perfect angel of a daughter was booted out.

I immediately replied, "If she is not listening and being disrespectful, then you have every right to treat her just like any other student. She deserved to be kicked out!"

The next class time, Tessa had moved to a different seat, but once again, because she did not follow directions, and after multiple requests from the teacher, she got kicked out of class. I had never known any kid with Down syndrome to be kicked out of their first two classes in the school year. But she did!

Fast-forward one week, and she was as happy as could be. The teacher said that she became happy and interactive with her peers once they started cooking and baking. Apparently, she was just bored with the first few classes of the school year and did not want to listen to the teacher's lecture. Tessa was only in class to bake ... and eat!

## Emma is a sixteen-year-old with Down syndrome.

Emma loves everything about being in high school. She loves her teachers and her friends. She loves walking (and running) down the hallways and being social. Part of her day includes working in some of the departments for some of the teachers a few days per week. She works in the history department and has become friends with the entire history department. She shreds, cleans offices, puts books away, and delivers mail. Whatever it is, she does it all with a smile. But she wants something in return for doing her job—candy—and makes certain all staff are aware. She has become so accustomed to doing work and "earning" a piece of candy at the end of her shift that every history teacher now has a bag of candy in their desk drawer specifically for my daughter.

One day, after completing her jobs, a few of the teachers noticed that the large Costco bags of candy were missing from their drawers. They also could not find Emma. She usually heads back to the main history office to get her candy, but she was not there. The teachers went looking for her and even texted and called her, but there was no answer. One of the teachers heard a noise coming from the history department hallway closet and gathered the other teachers. As they all got in front of the closet door, they heard a voice laughing inside the closet and having a conversation with herself, saying, "I'm so lucky. I'm hiding, and they can't find me."

The teachers opened the door and found Emma inside the closet lying on the ground with four opened bags of candy and about thirty candy wrappers surrounding her. She had chocolate on her face and hands. The teachers laughed hysterically, and my daughter's response was, "I need to go to the bathroom!"

## Sophie is a seventeen-year-old with Down syndrome.

I never know what Sophie will say at the end of each school day. Sophie came home one day and said, "Mom, I had a great day at school. I didn't steal anything today!" I could not have been prouder of her at that moment and will take that as a parenting win!

Another day, I picked up Sophie from school and asked her how her day was, and she said, "Leave me alone. You ask too many questions, and now I have a headache."

## Caroline is an eighteen-year-old with Down syndrome.

I received a call from my daughter's school nurse, who told me Caroline swallowed her hoop earring. In the background, I could hear Caroline crying and saying, "Mom is gonna be so mad at me. I don't want to talk to her."

The nurse put Caroline on the phone with me, and I asked, "Why did you swallow your earring?"

She first said, "I was hungry," and "You woke me up too early this morning, and I did not have time to finish my cereal."

We went to get an x-ray to make sure that the hoop had not punctured her insides or caused any damage. When she got her hospital gown on, she proceeded to twerk and began singing. I think she thought this was the start of a party, and she would not have to return to school. When the doctor came in to take her for the x-ray, she said, "I am not done twerking. Just give me a minute."

A few hours later, Caroline returned to school and was super excited about sharing the x-ray with her teachers and friends, which showed her hoop earring in her intestines.

After a few days of lots of movement and plenty of fluids, the hoop earring came out on its own, and Caroline never wore the earring again!

# The Working Life: A Comedy of Errors

**Jen is a twenty-year-old with Down syndrome.**

One of Jen's jobs was working at a daycare center where she would help the little kids with cleaning up, washing hands, getting their snacks, and putting on their coats at the end of the day. After that job eventually ended, she confessed to her older sister that when she used to hand out the snacks to the preschool children, she would take the snacks, go hide in a closet by herself, and eat them. She was stealing the preschoolers' snacks! We never heard of it until after the program ended, but she was very open about taking the snacks from the kids! Our beautiful, smart daughter was a thief!

**Jeff is a nineteen-year-old with Down syndrome.**

As Jeff became more independent, he started working a job. Unfortunately, he was unable to navigate public transit on his own. We would often get a cab to take him instead. One day I got a phone call from Jeff while on his way to his job on Devon Avenue in Chicago. He told me he thought the cab driver didn't know where he was going. I asked him where he was and if he could give me a location.

He responded, "In the cab."

After his very specific answer, I asked again, and he responded that he was about forty-five minutes from O'Hare International Airport, nowhere close to work. Following that incident, we took a break from riding independently to educate ourselves and Jeff more about transportation.

## Demetri is a nineteen-year-old with Down syndrome.

When at work, Demetri can eat lunch, which his employer provides. There are large serving pans filled with food that everyone can enjoy. Demetri decided to take his own spoon, and he inserted it into a huge pan of rice and began eating out of the pan. The employer had to throw out the entire pan of rice after seeing Demetri eat directly out of it! Needless to say, he never did that again!

## Demetri is a nineteen-year-old with Down syndrome.

Demetri started working at Culver's. He loved French fries, and one day while working, he decided to head back to the kitchen to eat some. Once the restaurant manager found out about the incident, I received a letter reprimanding Demetri for putting his hand in the public bin of French fries because it was a health issue. When asked why he took the French fries, he simply said, "I was hungry."

During another shift at Culver's, Demetri was delivering meals to a customer in the car line and kept smelling the delicious fries in the customer's bag. He thought, *I'm hungry*, and took a few from the bag. The customer witnessed what Demetri and and reported it to management. Demetri was reminded not to eat from the customers' bags anymore. Although he was reprimanded, he continues to remain employed because the staff loves him so much.

## Sophie is a seventeen-year-old with Down syndrome.

Sophie was starting a new job working at a hotel. She had attended some new employee training with her job coach, who would be on-site with her. After the final training session, Sophie was sent home with a few pages of rules and expectations regarding the new hotel job. The morning prior to her first day working at the hotel, I started to go over the expectations with her, and she put her hand up in front of my face and said, "Mom, you are talking too much and giving me a headache. I know what to do!"

## Jenna is a seventeen-year-old with Down syndrome.

Jenna has a huge sweet tooth, and if she had the opportunity to eat sweets all day long, she would. So, when her high school vocational counselor informed us that there was another opportunity for her to work in the community, we were excited. When we found out that the job would be working at a Crumbl cookie store, my husband and I both hit the pause button! We thought to ourselves, *She will never have the self-control to work there.* However, we eventually agreed because we thought it would be a great opportunity since she enjoyed baking, and the added skills she would learn would certainly outweigh the concern we had about her eating the raw cookie dough (because who doesn't like eating cookie dough?).

Day one was a total success. She followed directions, cleaned dishes, and followed all hygiene and safety expectations. At the end of any employee's shift, they receive one free cookie. These cookies are very large. We had instructed the vocational counselor that Jenna would be able to earn one cookie at the end of every workweek. Otherwise, she would receive three large cookies in one week, and although that would have made Jenna happy, her stomach would not agree with that decision.

At the end of her first shift, the manager generously allowed Jenna to take three cookies with her! This was the best work environment ever as far as Jenna was concerned. She called me to tell me about her day and that she got three free cookies: one for Mom, one for Dad, and one for her brother. I told her she was lucky, that I was proud of her, and that I would see her at home—and to bring all three cookies home. I immediately emailed the vocational teacher and reminded her that she was to earn only one cookie at the end of every workweek. Otherwise, Jenna would eat too much and get a stomach ache.

Twenty minutes later, Jenna called me again and asked if she could have a "small corner" of one of the cookies she was bringing home since she had a great day. I agreed. Thirty minutes later, I received a phone call from the school nurse telling me that Jenna was in her office complaining about a stomach ache. She said she had no temperature and seemed fine but wanted me to know. I told her earlier that day Jenna had begun working at Crumbl. She laughed.

I giggled to myself and rolled my eyes knowing exactly why she had a stomach ache. After being put on the phone with her, she immediately told me, "I'm sorry. I ate all three cookies. They were just so big and so good. I had to eat them."

**Maria is a twenty-one-year-old with Hurler syndrome.**

Maria was going to start an internship program. She was told the company she'd be working with was called Concordia Advisory Board, or CAB. When we asked about what she would be doing, she kind of shrugged it off and said, "I don't know. They have me working for a cab company!"

# Hygiene Follies

**Elizabeth is a twenty-three-year-old with Hurler syndrome.**

Elizabeth was attending college and was surprising us with how successfully she was navigating all the non-academic elements of college life in her freshman year. She was living with a roommate in a supportive environment, including an aide who was also living on the floor with them and some other students with special needs.

When she came home for fall break, she shared how much fun she was having and how much she was enjoying college. We let her know how proud of her we were and how we hoped she would continue to enjoy college. At the end of the weekend, we drove her back to campus and said our goodbyes.

On Tuesday morning, we noticed her toothbrush was on the counter in the bathroom in our home instead of with her at school. We called her and asked if she had been brushing her teeth since she had returned to school. She exclaimed, "Of course I have been brushing my teeth!"

We then asked how she was brushing her teeth. She said, "I just used my roommate's toothbrush because I couldn't find mine."

### Ben is a thirteen-year-old with cerebral palsy and hypomyelination.

Some days are just harder than others. Ben is thirteen and loves monster trucks and Grave Digger trucks. He's also incontinent. One morning I was changing him, and there was a bowel movement. I was praying his Grave Digger truck, which was still moving around the room while my son was being changed on the mat, didn't drive through his pile of poop. Needless to say, Grave Digger found the pile of poop on the floor and drove right through it. My son thought it was very funny and kept repeating the words, "Poop is funny. Poop is funny!"

### Autumn is an eighteen-year-old with Down syndrome ... and is also a liar!

Autumn and I were driving home from a doctor's appointment, and I heard a noise that sounded like a massive fart coming from Autumn. I looked at her and asked if she farted, and she said with a smile, "No, it wasn't me."

I told her to say "Excuse me" when she does that. She said again that it was not her and that it was her water bottle that was making loud fart noises. She then said it was her brother who farted. Her brother was not even in the car when it happened! She then started hysterically laughing and opened the window!

### Ryan is a twelve-year-old with Down syndrome.

Ryan was twelve years old and singing to himself while in the shower. He was in the bathroom for a long time when, all of a sudden, we heard him screaming. "Ow ow ow ow ow." We checked on Ryan and realized he picked up one of the razors in the shower and began to shave his upper lip, cutting himself very badly! There was no mirror in the shower to see what he was doing. He just figured he wanted to shave his upper lip, so he did it! He now uses an electric razor with assistance from his parents.

### David is a sixteen-year-old with Down syndrome and autism.

My son had been practicing shaving prior to his sophomore year. One school day, I received a message from his school stating, "It's really nice to see David has learned how to shave, but we would recommend keeping the razor at home." He was walking down the hallway to class while shaving his face when his caseworker heard a buzzing sound. From then on, we made sure David's backpack did not include an electric razor!

### Tessa is a seventeen-year-old with Down syndrome.

Tessa does not like it when I help her groom (pluck) her eyebrows. Each time, we need to talk about the process, what is going to happen, and that it is uncomfortable but that it needs to be done. On the day we were going to begin, she said, "I am not sure where the tweezers are." Since the tweezers are kept in my bathroom, I was confused since I did not move them. She then said, "I think Liam took them." I explained that I did not think her brother took her tweezers and that she was the only person who used them. I asked her if she moved them.

She said, "No."

I told her we needed to go to my bathroom to begin.

She said, "I think someone moved them in the garden. You won't ever find them." This did not make any sense because we did not have a garden. She did not want to get her eyebrows plucked, so she took her tweezers and hid them. After a few more rounds of back and forth, I told her she needed to tell me where the tweezers were.

She then said, "I am not sure where they are, but I will find them." She went outside, and in between two large bushes, she just happened to find her bright pink tweezers. She eventually caved and told me she threw the tweezers out of her bedroom window.

**Mike is a four-year-old with autism. His nickname became Houdini following his attempts at escaping his crib.**

At a certain age, Mike began to climb out of his crib. Concerned for his safety, I bought a crib tent, which is basically a mesh tent that goes over the top of the crib and unzips from the outside. It worked like a charm to keep him from escaping. However, not long after that, he began to escape from his clothing (and sometimes diaper) at night. One night, my husband and I were out, and our babysitter, Karoline, put Mike to bed. About an hour later, he was still awake and making noise, so she went in to check on him. What she discovered would be enough to make most babysitters change professions immediately.

Mike was completely naked, standing in his crib, and had apparently been playing Picasso with the contents of his diaper all over himself, the crib, and the tent. I'm pretty sure that's where the phrase "shit show" came from. Poor Karoline handled it like a champ. She cleaned up Mike's art studio and didn't even quit her job afterward. In fact, she was with us for another five years. The experience even inspired her to devise a genius way to keep Houdini from going commando at night. She sewed a button at the top of his one-piece romper pajamas and attached a small elastic hairband from the button to the zipper, which made them Mike-proof. Although it was Mike's first and final masterpiece, it is forever memorable.

# Love, Sex, and Disability

**James is a twenty-year-old with Down syndrome.**

James got a great special needs education through our public school system. We decided to supplement his sex ed education with an eight-week course taught to special needs children regarding boundaries and acceptable behavior. During the last session, the instructors were very careful because they said they were going to talk about what is now LGBTQ+, but at the time it was basically divided into heterosexual and homosexual relationships. They asked the parents and guardians if we were okay with them teaching the topic. We told them James has gay cousins, but I'm not sure if he completely understands what it means.

So after the last session, James walked out of the classroom and announced in a loud voice, "Hey, Dad, I'm straight."

I replied, "Yeah, James, we knew a long time ago you were straight, but you go, guy!"

**Jenna is a nineteen-year-old with Down syndrome.**

My daughter, Jenna, was taking part in a disability sexual education class. The most recent class was about body parts. I shared with her the PowerPoint before she went to class just to prepare her. She looked at the slides and then said, "Oh my God, that's so disgusting. Penises are gross."

After the class, she got into the car with a very big smile on her face. I asked her how the class went. She said, "It was awesome. I know about eggs and perm [sperm]. I know what a condom is and that when penises are hard, babies are born!"

## Steve is a nineteen-year-old with Down syndrome.

We were out to dinner one night with Steve's mother and brother, Alex, and Steve turned to me to say he learned something that day. He proceeded to share that when the penis gets hard, you always put a condom on it. You never have sex without a condom. Then he showed me with his index finger very straight how you put a condom on. I was trying to stay calm in the crowded restaurant, and I turned to his mom and said, "Hey, Mom. Steve learned something at school today."

"Well, what did you learn?" she asked.

At that point, Alex leaned in to see what Steve was sharing, and Steve very proudly turned to his mother to repeat what he had just shared with me. This triggered Alex to start giggling, so my wife executed a perfect NHL check on Alex, knocking him off the bar stool into the table—a move that would've made ESPN's nightly Top 10.

Alex was a little stunned by what happened, and while we picked him up and dusted him off, we told him we would not tolerate making fun of Steve learning the right things to do when practicing safe sex. A hilarious moment.

## Hannah is a nineteen-year-old with Down syndrome.

Hannah was signed up for a body, heart, and mind class for individuals with disabilities. The class focused on communication; relationship building; how to communicate with peers, boyfriends, and girlfriends; and even had a little sex education mixed in.

Following one recent class, Hannah exited the building with a huge smile on her face. I had viewed the curriculum prior to class starting and knew the content might be a little over her head as they were going to be discussing specific body parts and what they do. That didn't seem to bother her.

When I asked her how her class was, her smile got bigger, and she screamed, "It was amazing! I know what an anus is!"

# Disability in the Community

**Max is a nineteen-year-old with Down syndrome. He is never at a loss for words and enjoys embarrassing his mom!**

About one year ago Max and I were in the checkout line at Walmart. Maybe one person was ahead of me, and Max decided to grab something to drink from one of the coolers. I told him to make it quick. A few minutes later, I started unloading my stuff and was looking for him. I was getting irritated because there were now three people behind me. And now I was almost screaming, "Max, get your drink and get back here right now!" I apologized to the cashier and asked her to ring up one bottle of Coke.

She said, "I'm really sorry, but I have to actually use the barcode scanner to scan the drinks."

At that point, I was yelling out loud, "Max, get your butt over here right now! We have people waiting in line." And I saw him leisurely walking over to me like there was no rush.

So the drink was scanned, and Max turned around to face the long line and said, "I'm really sorry about my mom. She gets really agitated easily." I could not believe that he said that to the line of people waiting. After I had private words with him (yelling at him), he apologized to the people for keeping them waiting.

## Ben is a five-year-old with cerebral palsy and hypomyelination.

I always wrestle with myself as a parent about just how much to accommodate my son, who has a disability and is in a wheelchair. My son is a master negotiator. When he first got his wheelchair, he was not using his walker. He was around five when we really started to teach him about respecting his mom and dad, and if we told him not to go somewhere, he would listen.

We were at an outdoor mall, and I had to purchase an oven light at a store that was absolutely packed with people. I told him to stay put and not go (or "roll") anywhere. I walked away for a minute, looked back, and he was gone. I found him and reminded him to stay put and not "roll away." I walked away again, and when I looked back he was "hauling it" away from me.

I caught him and said, "You were warned." I lifted his wheels up from his wheelchair, as he was trying to push down, but he couldn't move. When he wouldn't listen, his wheels went up. I realized this was not the way to shop because he would not stop messing with the wheels. I threw him over my shoulder while he wailed and cried. I walked to the front of the store with the lightbulbs in one hand, my crying, hysterical son hanging over my shoulder, all while trying to navigate the wheelchair with my other hand.

I was sure the whole store was looking at me, thinking, "Who is that jerk of a dad?"

And I said, out loud to those looking at me and thinking likely negative things about me, "Look, even he has to follow the rules!"

## Dave is an eleven-year-old with autism.

My brother, Dave, who has autism and some other developmental disabilities, was not always able to communicate his feelings with words. One example of his ability to express his feelings without using words occurred when he was about eleven.

Like many families with loved ones with special needs, my mother would take my brother with her everywhere. She would say it was to expand his skills and give him greater exposure to the world. While there is some truth to that, the primary reason was to keep him safe and provide as much oversight as possible.

At least twice a week, they would make trips to the grocery store, and my mother would roam up and down every aisle, even if she didn't need anything in that aisle. On one occasion, when they were in the aisle with the chips and soft drinks, my brother planted himself and refused to continue snaking up and down the aisles. My mother figured he was safe in a large grocery store they visited frequently, so she proceeded with her shopping.

A few minutes later there was a loud *POW*, as if a small explosion had gone off. My mother scampered back to the snacks aisle where she had left my brother. She arrived at about the same time as the store manager and one of the staff who stocks the shelves. They found the floor soaked, and my brother's clothes were wet. They quickly surmised, and he later confirmed, that he had shaken a two-liter bottle of 7UP and then slammed it onto the floor. While he didn't know that it would explode, he was frustrated with the time it was taking to complete the grocery shopping, and he expressed his feelings with action.

The store manager was very kind and was only focused on my brother's well-being. He was fine, though his pants were soaked from the beverage bomb he detonated. My family increased their patronage of the store in the future, and my brother has gotten much better at using his words to express his emotions.

## Stuart is a nonambulatory six-year-old with cerebral palsy and autism, and Jake, his twin brother, also has autism.

We don't typically take everyone to the grocery store because it is challenging. Both of my sons have autism, and Jake was in a big stroller, Stuart was in a wheelchair, and their sister, Sarah, was with us. But during one grocery store visit, we were all waiting in line when Sarah, who was at the front of the line, turned around and said, "Mom, everybody's staring at me because I'm so cute!"

And I said, "Of course, that is why they are staring at you!"

## Tessa is a fourteen-year-old with Down syndrome.

"Tessa, Tessa? Where are you?" These were words that I have spoken often over the years, so it was not a total surprise to me that she had disappeared while we were shopping. Tessa has a knack for wandering. Not because she is angry or does not want to hang out with her family, but because she finds it hysterical and gets a kick out of hearing us (especially her mom) scream throughout the store, "Tessa, where are you? Tessa, come out now. Tessa this is not funny anymore."

Tessa has always been able to locate amazing hiding spots, whether in the back of our coat closet—so far back that it doesn't matter that coats had fallen off the hangers and lay on the closet floor. Tessa would find those fallen coats and hide under them and not be found. There was another time she hid inside our dryer. That was a bit frightening. She also disappears in between racks of clothing in stores. When she is finally found, she giggles and smiles and says, "I got you!" or "I am so funny!"

We were shopping at the local mall, and I took my eyes off her for what seemed like only a minute. That was plenty of time for Tessa to wander off. She was nowhere to be found. I searched the clothing racks, the dressing rooms, looked underneath pillows and cushions, and asked the staff if anyone had seen "the little girl with Down syndrome who was wearing a blue coat." I walked outside of the store and looked left then right—no Tessa. I could begin to feel my heart beat faster, and I was beginning to feel a bit queasy. I was ready to run to the other end of the mall when I happened to look at the store window display. I realized the girl with the blue coat who had Down syndrome was literally sitting in the display window smiling, dancing, and waving at people walking by the store.

My irritation with Tessa quickly softened as I smiled and waved back at her. She was so happy in that display case. Who could blame her—she found another great hiding spot!

## Caroline is a nineteen-year-old with Down syndrome.

I took Caroline Christmas shopping with me the other day. Ironically, the day I took her I was shopping FOR her. One might think that I would not be able to get away with actually taking her into the store and walking the aisles all while searching for holiday gifts for Caroline.

All I have to do is follow her, see what she likes, and remember the items. I then send her to the candy aisle to pick out ONE thing to eat, grab the liked items and head over to the checkout. As long as there is no line, I have plenty of time to pay, double bag the items, and head back to the candy aisle, where I know she will still be trying to decide which candy bar to buy. This is one perk of having a daughter with a disability!

She might ask, "What is in the bag?"

"Bath towels." My answer doesn't even matter because she is

so focused on the candy! Christmas is a lock this year!

## Sam is a forty-five-year-old with autism.

This started out as awkward but turned funny. I was leading a group of thirteen adults with disabilities to The Second City Laugh Factory on a Friday night. We sat down in our seats, and I saw a couple of people talking on stage. One of the actors waved me over and said, "I just wanted to talk to you ahead of time because there might be parts of this show that are not appropriate. We make fun of all different kinds of people in this show, and I just want to tell you there's a part where we make fun of people with disabilities."

*Okay, this is great,* I thought. *You know what? We're here. This is real life, and we are not going to leave.* She went on to tell me that she had a background in special education, so she wanted to tell us ahead of time. They got up there to do the skit, and I could just see the adults I was with were looking at me for permission to laugh. They all thought it was hysterical. The comedians were asking for volunteers from the audience, and we had a rather outspoken funny gentleman with our group named Sam, who raised his hand. I, along with other staff, was thinking, *Oh no, what is he going to say?!* He went up on stage, and the comedian who initially gave us the heads up was there so she was able to adapt it, and she made it hilarious for all of us!!

## Jackson is a twenty-year-old with autism.

One day while teaching at a high school, we took a group of our students to a store and walked around looking for items for a party. One of our students, Jackson, was with us and always had meltdowns. He would be the one in the middle of the store to have a meltdown and would always refuse to get up. On this particular visit, there happened to be a little kid having a tantrum on the floor. Jackson asked, "What's wrong with this kid? He needs to just get up."

Jackson approached the child, and the mother looked anxious and nervous about why this older kid was approaching her son. Jackson sat on the floor next to the kid, and we all wondered what was happening. Jackson talked to the kid for a short time, and he stopped crying. They were having a fun conversation.

Jackson looked up at me and said, "Why was this kid being so mean? I am so good, aren't I?"

## Demetri is a fifteen-year-old with Down syndrome.

A few years ago, our family attended a wedding at the Loews Hotel in Chicago. We were enjoying the night when I realized I had not seen Demetri in a while, and I started to panic. I began asking his siblings and security for assistance and if they had seen him. We noticed there was another wedding taking place across the hall. We opened the door and saw Demetri happily dancing with the bride at her wedding! We tried to coax Demetri away from this wedding, but the bride was having so much fun with him, and she wanted him to stay. The bride was so happy that Demetri crashed her wedding that she invited him to stay for cake!

Our only regret is that we wish we knew who the bride was because she was wonderful, and Demetri was having the best time!

## Autumn is a nineteen-year-old with Down syndrome.

Autumn has been going to the gym a few times a week for the past year. She loves it because she gets to do a lot of boxing and dancing. The owner created a playlist for her to listen to when the gym was not busy. My daughter had been working out one morning, and the gym got really busy. As a result, she was not able to continue listening to her music. So she literally stopped working out and did not move her body in the gym. She just stood in the gym with her gloves on looking down at the ground. We decided to ignore her and continue working out on our own. Several minutes went by when no one was paying attention to her, and she got angry. She proceeded to run out of the gym, found a large garbage can, and hit and boxed it, all while singing one of the songs from her own playlist very loudly!

Once she was done attacking the garbage can, she joyfully ran back into the gym and started dancing to the music that was playing.

## Tessa is a seventeen-year-old with Down syndrome.

Tessa went to the DMV with her mom to get an Illinois state ID disability card. We got there shortly after it opened, and there was already a line of what felt like one hundred people. We got in line behind the last person. Tessa did not want to wait in line and was becoming annoyed and agitated. I walked up to the front and asked the employee if they could make an exception. He informed me that she could jump to the senior/disability persons line, where no one was waiting. I went to get Tessa from the line, told her what was happening, and we proceeded to walk to the other line. As we walked, I could feel everyone's eyes on us and heard one girl say, "Where are they going?"

I turned around and, without thinking, replied, "It's my one disability perk. Get over it."

Tessa looked at me and then turned around and told the girl to "Suck it!"

# The Hilarious Adventures of Traveling With a Disability

**Olivia is a nonverbal fourteen-year-old quadriplegic who loves being in the water.**

Our friends have a vacation home in Wisconsin, and we all decided to go canoeing. My sister, Olivia, is autistic and in a wheelchair, but she loves the water. Olivia was on the dock waiting for us when we heard our family friend yelling for "help." While she was yelling for help, Olivia had rolled into the lake while still in her wheelchair, but we only heard joy and laughter coming from Olivia.

My dad and friend jumped into the water, grabbed her, and got her out of the water without her getting hurt. As terrified and upset as we all were at the time, she was still laughing after we got her out. Moving forward, we always make certain that the wheelchair is locked!

**Brett is a five-year-old with cerebral palsy.**

Our youngest son, Brett, was granted a wish through the Make-A-Wish Foundation when he was five. He wanted to go to a "good beach." We assured him that Hawaii had good beaches.

From the moment we arrived, our family spent a lot of time on the beach and playing in the waves. Several months after we arrived home, Brett finally told us that he couldn't hear very well. The doctor ordered a scope since he had no infection. The doctor was surprised to find sand in both of his ear canals, which had been stuck in his ears for three months!

Brett laughed. "I had Hawaii in my ears!"

## Ben is a thirteen-year-old with cerebral palsy and hypomyelination.

We travel to Philadelphia for all of Ben's medical appointments. We flew Delta on our recent trip. They are wonderful working with families who have kids with special needs. Ben enjoys traveling and is always happy and makes friends wherever he goes. We were running late and pushing his wheelchair to the gate, and the lines to board had already formed. This was during the winter, and there had been some storms. The winter weather made travel more difficult, so many passengers were annoyed and angry because they had been delayed. We went to the gate, and before we could even say anything, the employee looked at us, and Ben, and said, "Don't worry. I got you." She checked us in, and we were able to bypass the long line of people waiting to board. We started moving and smiling at the other passengers in line, grateful that we did not have to wait.

Ben was smiling and said very loudly, "See you later, suckers. Sorry about your wait time!" I proceeded to push his wheelchair much faster and kept my head down so as not to piss off anyone else!

## Anna is an eight-year-old with Down syndrome.

When Anna was eight, our family visited Las Vegas for a wedding. Because she was a minor, she was not allowed by the slot machines. As we entered the hotel, we followed the red carpet that went straight through the casino to the elevators. Anna was all dressed up in her brightly colored tutu and ballet shoes and proceeded to pirouette her way through the casino. She decided to stop at every slot machine with someone playing, tap them on their shoulder, and say, "Good luck!" She pirouetted her way through the casino for the next twenty minutes wishing the slot players good luck. Security was watching, and although she was a minor, they were hysterically laughing and allowed her to proceed through the casino! Because, seriously? Who is going to stop an adorable eight-year-old with Down syndrome wearing a tutu from walking through the casino and making guests happy?

**Michael is a twenty-four-year-old with autism.**

On an overnight trip in Maine we had a group of about twenty-five adult participants with special needs hiking up a mountain. About halfway up the mountain a participant, Michael, who I was walking next to, said, "You ever have that feeling that you're going to blow out your shorts?"

I said, "Yeah. Does your stomach hurt?"

He said, "Something is going on down there, and I have to get rid of it!" Suddenly, he said, "Well, that just happened!" So we went off the hiking trail into the woods, found the biggest leaves we could, cleaned up with them, and rinsed with some water from his water bottle. He then proceeded to move on and finished the hike like a total rockstar!

**Dan is a fourteen-year-old with Down syndrome.**

One Christmas we stayed at a nice resort in Maui. One night we went to a luau that featured belly dancers. Around this time, Dan was fourteen and discovering his hormones. As the dancers came out, he announced, "Here comes the hips." The phrase has now become a family saying whenever Dan fancies a lady.

### Stephen is a twenty-one-year-old with Down syndrome.

My brother, Stephen, likes plays and musicals and is always asking us to take him to see a show. He has been to New York City to see a few shows already. A few years ago, my husband and I took him to New York City for the weekend, and I got tickets to see a show. Even though they were very expensive, I knew he would be thrilled to see a play. The seats were at the very top of the theater. Instead of thanking me, he said, "You know I prefer to sit in the orchestra!"

### Stephen is a fourteen-year-old with Down syndrome.

My family and I were on a guided tour while on vacation in Hawaii. The guide thought my brother, Stephen, was really smart and funny, so she asked him, "What is your favorite island?"

My brother replied, "Rhode Island!"

### Anna is an eight-year-old with Down syndrome.

When Anna was eight, we visited Las Vegas for a wedding. We opted for the one-day buffet, where we paid one fee and could go back and eat any time of the day. For five days, Anna had pizza for lunch and dinner. Anna's favorite food is pizza. One morning, Anna and I went to the buffet for breakfast. There were only older people there because everyone else was still asleep. Every breakfast item was available on the buffet tables. Anna was walking around the buffet tables looking for something to eat. From the other side of the restaurant, Anna yelled at the top of her lungs, "Where is the pizza?"

I walked up to her and said, "It's breakfast. There is no pizza."

Anna replied, "This is bullshit," and walked away. She could not understand why her favorite food was not part of the breakfast buffet at seven o'clock in the morning. Unfortunately, that morning, she had to settle for cereal.

## Jackson is a six-year-old with autism.

For years we've spent weekends at our family's lake house in southern Wisconsin. Jackson has always loved the water, and one summer, it seemed like he wanted to be in it constantly. We had a life jacket on him and would wade with him in the shallow water. He would stay by us, but eventually he would drift out to deeper water, and we'd have to retrieve him. After repeatedly chasing him, my husband and I came up with the brilliant idea of tying a ski rope to the pier and the other end through the back loop of Jackson's life jacket. That way Jackson could venture out on his own, and we could stay dry on the pier watching him enjoy himself without having to constantly retrieve him. I'm not going to lie: the thought did cross my mind as to how it must have looked to other boaters, etc., seeing this young child in the water on a "leash" tied to a pier. One of our finer moments as parents, for sure.

## Brett is a three-year-old with cerebral palsy.

Our family had to travel across the country for our son to have two brain surgeries. We stayed at the Ronald McDonald House in Orange County, California. Our three-year-old son, Brett, was forced to sleep in what was called "the mother-in-law's" room, but it was really a closet with a bed!

## Anna is a sixteen-year-old with Down syndrome.

Anna always becomes excited when we talk about going out of town. She thinks each time we hop in the car on a road trip, it is a party. She will say, "I want to go to a hotel, have room service, eat cake, go swimming, and go in a hot tub." But this time, we were headed out of town for a family BBQ on a Saturday afternoon and only gone a portion of the day. She became very upset when we told her we were only headed to see family and not staying in a hotel.

She said, "I don't want to visit family. Can't you just drop me off at the hotel and pick me up tomorrow?"

We all just rolled our eyes!

## Hannah is a sixteen-year-old with Down syndrome.

Our family took a spring break trip to Las Vegas last year. We landed without incident and got to our hotel without any issues. We were waiting in line to check in and realized Hannah was nowhere in sight. We had lost her—again! When she wandered in the past, we were not overly concerned because she remained in her natural environment. We had just arrived at this huge hotel, and it was extremely crowded. We began our search of Hannah. We found a security guard and gave him a description of the little girl with pink sneakers who had Down syndrome. A second later, I heard, "MOM!" I turned and saw Hannah. She was sitting in a chair trying to play the slot machines. She was smiling, happy and very proud of herself that she found the machines without anyone's help! She then said, "Can I have money?"

## Sam is a two-year-old with Down syndrome.

Sam was about two years old when we took a family trip to Disney World. At the time, they still had the red pass, which would allow anyone with a disability to jump to the front of the line. We had the red pass in our hands, but I felt guilty using it to bypass the line. My other kids wanted to go on the Aladdin ride, but the line was over two hours long. I still was conflicted about using the pass, and my wife and I were discussing whether we should or should not use it. Finally, my wife said, "This is one of the only disability perks we will ever get. Let's play the card!"

So, we used the pass, jumped to the front of the line, and my eldest son at the time said to Sam, "Thank you for having Down syndrome!"

## Sam is an eighteen-year-old with Down syndrome.

When Sam was a senior in high school, our family visited a friend's lake house. The rules were a little more flexible, and parents permitted their older teenagers to enjoy a few light alcoholic drinks like hard seltzers. Since Sam was eighteen, he also participated in having a drink. A few pictures were taken of everyone enjoying themselves, and Sam had a picture taken with friends as he held his seltzer.

Fast-forward to the fall, as I was putting together our family holiday card, I added the picture of Sam with the alcoholic drink in his hand. I did not even think about the fact that he was under the legal drinking age when I was putting the card together. The family card was sent to all our family and friends, including the family who owned the lake house. The daughter of the family, who is Sam's age and also a senior, recognized that it was her backyard and then proceeded to share our family card with all of her friends because she thought it was cool that Sam was drinking in her backyard. He became the talk of the lunchroom and an even cooler kid to many around school!

# Celebrations: When Disability and Chaos Collide

**Aaron is a forty-seven-year-old with Down syndrome.**

Aaron is known to rip apart the wrapping paper on his gifts to see what's inside without waiting. Once he figures out what the gift is, he doesn't spend much time admiring it but is ready to be given the next present and begin ripping the paper off.

Last Christmas, I mistakenly didn't explain to him that my brother's Black Panther Marvel figure was not a gift, and the box didn't need to be treated as gift wrapping, but rather something cool to show the biggest Marvel fan in our family. As soon as I handed him the figure in the original box (which is important in the collector world), he began to rip the box apart to get to the small figure. He briefly glanced over the figure and was no longer interested. He placed it on the coffee table and tossed the shredded box to the ground.

**Tessa is a ten-year-old with Down syndrome.**

Tessa's favorite candy is a Kit Kat bar. She loves them, and when eating them, she will even sing the theme song, "Give me a break, give me a break, break me off a piece of that Kit Kat bar." Her friends and family are fully aware this is her favorite candy.

When it was time to open her birthday presents, she could not have been happier. Along with gift cards, slippers, silly string, and a few pieces of jewelry, she received ten king-size Kit Kat bars. She was in heaven, and upon opening the gift, she could not comprehend why we would not allow her to eat every single candy bar.

She said, "I am ten. I can do whatever I want!" She tried a few different times to sneak the candy into her pockets and eventually her room, but we caught on very quickly and took them away.

Fortunately, Halloween is the day after her birthday, so we were able to put most of the birthday candy into the Halloween candy bucket and give it out without her knowing!

## Sophie is an eight-year-old with Down syndrome.

Every few months, my boss and his family come over for dinner, and Sophie gets very excited knowing that they always "make it rain" candy when they arrive. This evening was no different. She saw them pull up and ran from the back of the house to the front and said, "Hi, guys." They attempted to talk with Sophie and engage in conversation before the "big reveal," but she knew what to expect and preferred less chit-chat and more time for eating candy. All she could focus on was the candy she knew was coming. She was also not shy about communicating this sentiment to them.

She interrupted them and said, "What is behind your back? Make it rain, make it rain, make it rain!" They eventually obliged by pulling out a baggie full of Hershey's Kisses and throwing a handful in the air. Sophie's excitement grew as they fell to the ground. She screamed with joy and began frantically unwrapping and eating every piece of candy, leaving the wrappers scattered on the ground for her mom to pick up. When I asked her to help her mom pick up the wrappers, she held up her chocolate-smeared hands and said, "Sorry, I am busy eating and can't help you. Do it yourself!"

## Emma is an eighteen-year-old with Down syndrome.

On the first night of Hanukkah, Emma was super excited to open a gift. It took her about fifteen minutes to decide which present to open. She quickly unwrapped the gift, threw the paper aside, opened the box, and said, "This gift sucks. I should have opened the other box."

## Liam is an eight-year-old with Down syndrome.

We are Korean and have over fifty cousins. My father passed away on Christmas Eve, and every year we have a memorial for him. It is sad, but it's also Christmas, an exciting time, and we follow the Korean tradition. We set up a table with different types of food and add our personal touches, which is what my dad would like. With the tradition, my dad's spirit is supposed to come down and be able to be with our family. The family takes turns bowing and kneeling in front of my dad's picture. We light a candle, pour wine, say something about my dad, and kiss the picture. There are lots of tears and emotions as we all share in this tradition.

Liam figured out the routine and started doing it several times in a row. He knew that the family would give him attention and praise as a result. He even started fake crying to get more attention! Even in a sad situation, he knows how to make people happy!

**Tessa is an eighteen-year-old with Down syndrome.**
Tessa had been talking about going skydiving since her older sister jumped last year. For her eighteenth birthday, we planned to take her skydiving. In preparation for the big jump, she wanted to practice. I told her there really was no way to practice jumping out of an airplane, but she insisted. After breakfast the day before her scheduled jump, she went to the backyard and stood on a bench. She then put her arms up in the air and jumped off the bench, landing on the ground with her hands still in the air. She then looked at me and said, "I am ready to jump!" If only it were that easy!

# Performances That Were Not Always Award Winning

**Liam is an eighteen-year-old with autism who loves being on stage!**

During one of our Special Gift Theatre final performances of *The Lion King*, one of the actors who had just walked off the main stage accidentally left his microphone on. While backstage, Liam could not control his impulses and continued to recite other people's lines while they were on stage performing. Liam had amazing recall and was able to recite not only his lines but also remembered other actors' lines. He basically was reciting the entire play from memory! The funny part was the audience could hear him reciting the lines and the teachers attempting to turn off his microphone and allow the other actors on stage to perform without interruption. Eventually, Liam allowed the teachers to turn off his microphone but only after he took a bow backstage!

**Jason is a twenty-one-year-old with Down syndrome.**

We hosted the All Camp Talent Show, and everyone from the surrounding towns came together for it. We had a camper named Jason who loved being onstage and in the spotlight but, to our surprise, did not do anything for the talent show. The MC was one of the camp directors, and the show was kind of boring. There was no excitement. Jason kept screaming out, introducing everyone, and he was trying to get up on stage. The staff kept telling him, "No, you cannot."

But during the middle of the show, he was so excited and could not sit in his seat. Jason got up on stage, started talking to everyone, and got the whole crowd excited about being at the show. He started announcing the rest of the talent show, which changed the entire program, including the evening program! He was cracking jokes and having fun. I haven't seen that much excitement at camp for a really long time.

The funny part was the staff tried to keep him from going up there. But they could see the MC was not very good and didn't seem to be having a fun time on stage. As soon as Jason came up and grabbed the mic, she stayed back and just let him go! It was awesome. I've never seen such excitement around the talent show. And all we did was include Jason and trust him and his instincts. There was so much laughter! It is great when everyone can just let go and give everyone time to shine when they can. It's okay when things don't go how you think they should go. In the end, it was so much better—the absolute best talent show!

**Aaron is a fifteen-year-old with autism and cerebral palsy.**

Aaron could spend all day with old VCR tapes. He's pretty specific about what he likes and would probably get rid of 99 percent of the movies because he didn't like them. If we really wanted to distract him, we would give him the whole container, and he could spend all day putting one in, watching a little bit of a video, and then taking it out, repeating the same thing over and over again. One day he found a movie and was so content and loved it. I figured I should go downstairs and see what he was watching. I went into his room and realized he was watching the Spice Girls movie! He was so happy watching the Spice Girls on a double-decker bus in London. It was also completely out of the norm for him to like something like this. When I told one of my friends that I found my son watching a Spice Girls video, they laughed and said, "It sounds like he knows what he wants, what he really, really wants!"

## Tessa is an eighteen-year-old with Down syndrome.

Tessa loves watching horror movies. She can watch the same scary movie repeatedly, so it was no surprise when she told me that she wanted to see the movie *Smile* for a second time. She said she was eighteen and wanted to see a movie by herself and eat popcorn. She saw it for the first time with her siblings, but they thought it was too scary and ended up on their phones the entire time, but Tessa loved it. There were even parts throughout the movie where I was told she laughed and giggled. She helped order her ticket online, and then we reminded her how to enter the theater and check in with her phone. We then reminded her to stand in line and only order a small popcorn. Once that was done, I followed her to the movie theater, where I showed her how to locate her seat. Once she was situated, I told her to text me when the movie was over and to wait for me in the lobby. After an hour and fifteen minutes, I received a text from Tessa saying, "Come pick me up. I want to get out of here now. It is too scary." I called her back, and she said she was "out of here" and "done with the movie." She told me it was too scary to see by herself. I picked her up and told her I was proud of her for being independent and going alone.

On the way home, she asked me, "Can I go back and see the movie again?"

## Joe is a twenty-two-year-old with Down syndrome.

Our participants played in a buddy basketball game a couple of years ago at Northwestern University, and the people in charge of the event were so nervous. They were concerned about how everything would work, making sure everyone was on time and that no one wandered away from the court.

Our participants sang the national anthem, and it went well. Then the halftime show was ready to begin. The people in charge gave us directions again and were clearly concerned about the participants following their directions. The players became very annoyed—they just wanted to go out on the court and play. A few of the players said, "Okay, we've got this. Just let us play now." They went out on the court, and they played. The organizers said they never had such a rowdy crowd before. The crowd was cheering us on, and so many funny, hilarious things were happening during the game.

At one point, Joe, who has Down syndrome, was running up and down the court just holding the ball. He became so excited when the crowd cheered for him that he stopped running, put the ball down, and took a bow in the middle of the court! The referees were allowing everyone several shots so that they could make a basket. They were actually playing their game of basketball and having the best time. They didn't have to be perfect. The crowd was fantastic, and all the administrators were so nervous for no reason!

## Tessa is an eleven-year-old with Down syndrome.

Tessa had been involved in Special Olympics swimming. We were thrilled when she got to participate in a swimming meet at Lake Forest College. She was hesitant at her event since she could not dive into the pool. Like many other athletes, she started her race in the pool. There was one other competitor. All other lanes were free.

Once the bell rang for the event to begin, Tessa started swimming, and the other participant did not. He chose not to move at all. Tessa continued to swim but got tired after about thirty seconds. She decided she was done competing. She slowly dog-paddled to the center where the swimming lane line was and began to hang on it. She then used the lane line to pull herself to complete the remainder of her event.

Because Tessa was the only participant in the water, they gave her a gold medal, even though she should have been disqualified!

**Brett is a fifteen-year-old with autism.**

Bella and Brett have participated in Special Olympics throughout high school and transition. Both of our families all sit together, rain or shine. Brett's event was always the last, and it was the "fast walking" event. We all lined up to watch him, and the coach told Brett, "You've got this, Brett. You're going to do great."

The gun went off, and off he went. Brett was winning by a good amount. Suddenly we looked, and I said, "What's he doing?" We all noticed Brett walking fast but was moving his arms up and down and side to side, and we realized that he was doing the movements to the "Macarena" song. He did this because he was happy that he was winning the race! He continued with his race and went right by us doing the "Macarena" with a big smile on his face. We were all on the sidelines roaring with laughter and approval! Brett did win the race!

**Taylor is a nonverbal fifteen-year-old with cerebral palsy and a history of seizures.**

Taylor is nonverbal, has cerebral palsy, and is very low functioning but loves music. Taylor's grandmother got him hooked on listening to Johnny Cash and got him *The Best of Johnny Cash* CD. He loves the songs "Folsom Prison Blues" and "Ring of Fire." If you put either of those songs on, Taylor lights up like a Christmas tree! He gets very excited and starts shaking his head back and forth in rhythm with the music.

## Tessa is an eleven-year-old with Down syndrome.

Tessa had been involved in Special Olympics track and field through her special recreation association. Tessa and her team went downstate to participate in the Illinois Special Olympic summer games, where she was to run the last leg of her relay race. It was rainy and cold. All the athletes looked cold and miserable from the bleachers where we were seated. Once Tessa's race started, the rain increased, and many families took cover, leaving their seats. Tessa received the baton from runner number three and began running the final leg of the relay race. As she ran past the bleachers, she slowed down, looked up at her family who remained in the stands and, with a huge smile on her face, waved at everyone. She then screamed, "I love you, Mom," and blew me a kiss.

The people in the stands laughed and cheered loudly for her to complete the race. Although they finished in last place, she crossed the finish line cold and wet but with a huge smile on her face and high-fived the volunteers.

## Brett is a fifteen-year-old with autism and is a fierce competitor!

Brett is a Special Olympic athlete, and his favorite event is the fast walking race that he has been involved in for years. Each year, Brett's biggest competitor in the event is a blind athlete, who is always inside the track on the far left because they have a rope for him to use. Over the years, they have been very competitive, trading off both gold and silver medals in this fast walking race.

During one race, the blind athlete was very fast, and they were tied at one point. Brett could see his competitor, and all of the sudden they were neck and neck. Brett pushed the blind competitor out of the way because he was creeping into his lane. Brett is so competitive that he just pushed him to the ground.

Brett's mother was mortified, screaming, "Oh my gosh. Oh my gosh," while the rest of Brett's family and friends laughed hysterically and almost wet their pants! The blind athlete was totally fine! Brett won the race but got disqualified because he pushed the other runner down.

Brett could not understand why he was disqualified and did not win the gold medal. He kept saying, "What do you mean? I don't understand. I won the race. I won the race."

**Stuart is a fifteen-year-old with cerebral palsy.**

Stuart would spend the weekends at his grandparents' house. And they would like to turn on *The Lawrence Welk Show* on Saturday nights. He loves all types of music and would get so excited, clapping his hands, smiling, moving back and forth in his chair. He would put his arms up in the air and love the music from the show!

We later found Lawrence Welk on YouTube, and he still watches it regularly. I never thought I would have a child who enjoyed watching and listening to Lawrence Welk over the Rolling Stones!

**Jane is a thirty-three-year-old with Down syndrome.**

We were on an overnight trip to Florida with a group of adults with disabilities. They had karaoke at the hotel. I know I'm not a good singer, so I never do karaoke (and I didn't that night), but some people don't care how they sound on stage, which is fantastic. Jane, one of our participants, said she wanted to sing, so she got up on stage. I supported her and said, "Yes, go ahead. You sing in the choir!"

We thought she was going on stage to sing a pop song, but she sang Captain and Tennille's "Do That to Me One More Time!" It was completely unexpected! Jane was fantastic. I mean, it was fantastically bad, but she didn't care. We all sat there laughing because there were people in the audience who looked very confused. Like, *What is going on right now? Am I being punked?*

They were not sure if it was okay to laugh at her singing and song choice. It was great because she gave us permission to laugh and have fun with it all.

IT'S OKAY TO LAUGH

# Acknowledgements

Oak Wealth Advisors is grateful for the relationships we have with our clients, colleagues, and friends throughout the disability community who encouraged us to pursue this project and shared their humorous stories with us. We hope that the stories we collected will put smiles on your faces as you read them. We loved the interactions we had while collecting the stories and hearing how much all the individuals in the stories are loved by their families.

We are also appreciative of the collaboration with Ryan Niemiller, who wrote the foreword for us. Ryan "gets it" and we could not be happier that he is enjoying a successful career as a world-class comedian who happens to have a disability.

The patience and support provided by Kristin Mitchell at Little Creek Press was essential in seeing this project to its conclusion. Kristin understood our vison for sharing stories and was very reassuring when doubts crept into our thinking.

# About The Authors

**Mike Walther**

Mike's brother, Sean, inspired him to start Oak Wealth Advisors in 2008. Mike cherishes all the humorous life experiences he has shared with his brother, and he is immensely proud of all his brother's accomplishments. Mike's career mission is to assist other families with loved ones with disabilities with their financial planning so that they can live their best lives.

**Randi Gillespie**

Randi's daughter, Maddy, exudes the silliness found throughout the book. Her Down syndrome is just one part of who she is. Randi works tirelessly to provide inclusion and opportunities for her daughter and others throughout the country as the Oak Wealth Advisors Director of Special Needs Services.

Printed in the United States
by Baker & Taylor Publisher Services